7TH TIME LUCKY

7TH TIME LUCKY

*One Gay Man's Determination to Become
a Parent*

David Rigby

Book Guild Publishing

Sussex, England

First published in Great Britain in 2014 by
The Book Guild Ltd
The Werks
45 Church Road
Hove, BN3 2BE

Typesetting in Garamond by
Nat-Type, Cheshire

Printed and bound in Great Britain by
CPI Group (UK) Ltd, Croydon, CR0 4YY

A catalogue record for this book is available from
The British Library.

ISBN 978 1 84624 956 3

Contents

CONTENTS

CONTENTS

Introduction

At the point when I knew I was going to embark on an unpredictable journey through surrogacy to see if I could bring a child into this world, I started to write. I didn't write for an audience, I wrote just in case something fantastic actually arrived in my life at the end of that journey.

I knew that if a child was brought into this world, that child would have to find out how he or she arrived. I didn't want to have to make up any stories about how they arrived. I wanted to be able to tell the story of the positive process I went through, the fun I had along the way, the supportive people I encountered, the fantastic woman who carried my child, and the moment that child arrived in my arms. I always knew that I would be honest with my child about how he or she arrived, about having two dads and not having a mum, and about how they were as loved as any other child in the world. I wanted that child to be able to read about all the steps I went through in bringing a new life into this world.

Now, saying I was a bit over-optimistic at the outset would probably win the prize for over-statement of the century. The ups and downs, highs and lows, heartache, lies, disappointments (and there were many) are all included. I hope that my daughter enjoys reading this account of how she came to be, and I also hope she realises just how much having a child really meant to me.

Some Background ...

Growing up through my teenage years and into young adulthood, I always knew I was gay, or at least that I was attracted to men rather than women. I didn't know early on how to classify this, but I knew that I was different from the general expectation of a Catholic boy growing up in a backwards little village in Lancashire. Freckleton was full of 'normal' people who passionately promoted having 'normal' lives. Anything else was to be severely frowned upon, and regularly was.

It probably wasn't until my sister's wedding in the early nineties that I suddenly realised that being this way inclined, I would never have a wedding day and that did upset me. In fact I cried my way through most of the evening reception – probably as much to do with the beer I was drinking as the emotion of it all. Sadly I hadn't told anyone about my sexuality at the time, so had to make up some lame excuse about why I was upset. What hadn't really registered at that point was that, not being straight or having any realistic prospect of getting married, I wouldn't ever be a dad.

Seeing my sister raise her children (albeit from a distance – I was either in London or she was in America) and seeing other relatives, friends and colleagues have their families, I was pretty much always hit by how envious I was. These people were able to create a life and their own families, and have a reason to live other than going to work, having a social life and paying for expensive nights out, cars, houses, clothes, holidays (and partners!).

I think I had known early on that I would never go through the whole pretend relationship or marriage thing. I had lots of girlfriends when I was young, too many really, but it always felt as though I was going through the motions just for the sake of it. I never totally enjoyed being with them as I felt I should have done (although some of them turned out to be good friends) and although the sex was do-able and sometimes enjoyable, it never left me feeling totally fulfilled or totally satisfied. I don't think the thought of pretending to be straight and making a commitment to a life-long relationship with a woman ever really entered my head once I knew what my sexuality was and I was comfortable with it. My own personal morals really couldn't have coped with it either and I would have hated reaching the point where I wanted to live my life as who I really was rather than as some faker.

In my twenties and through to my thirties, I still always thought I would have loved to have children: someone to love for the rest of my life and care for, and enjoy life with. I never really thought this was something I would get from a partner in a gay relationship. My expectations of gay men, even at that stage, were pretty low in terms of honesty, commitment and the longevity of any relationship. I'd realised pretty quickly that stability in any gay relationship is pretty rare and I put this down to the whole honesty thing – most gay men just aren't and I'd found this out in some unfortunate circumstances throughout my life. I knew I was by no means perfect though, so I had no real right to judge anyone else. I was just being realistic to a certain extent.

Samantha

When I was in my early thirties, I'd been in a relationship with Darren for about six or seven years and I was working as HR Manager for a company in Fleetwood. After a while, at the point where I was starting to manage a takeover of staff from another company, I was introduced to Samantha, a manager within that company with whom I was going to have to work quite a lot over the coming months. She was about to come and work with me and was going to be in charge of setting up some new teams for which I would manage the recruitment.

She and I hit it off straight away and quite quickly we were able to have a laugh and a joke, to the point where we ended up socialising outside of work. She met Darren and we all got on, and we had her and her fiancé, Simon, round to the house a couple of times. It was fun to be around her and we enjoyed each other's company.

Samantha and I had a lot in common. My relationship with Darren was fast heading down the pan. Sex was practically non-existent; if anything ever did happen, it was always because I made the effort and this was never, ever reciprocated. The relationship was more about companionship than anything else and I needed so much more. Although I had tried on numerous occasions to tackle it, and Darren agreed on every occasion to try and change, nothing ever worked. This just left me more and more frustrated and I began to wonder if it was worth continuing. I didn't know what else I could do to improve the situation apart from leave. My self-esteem and self-confidence couldn't take the constant hits.

Samantha and Simon were practically in the same boat. They were planning their wedding for the following summer; the venues were booked and guest lists written, but she just wasn't happy and found Simon too boring to be able to stomach the prospect of a long and happy future with him. I think it was our respective situations that brought us quite close.

The Christmas after we first met, Samantha and I had decided we would head to Manchester to do some Christmas shopping and this was where it all started. We had made a half-hearted attempt at shopping, but after probably half an hour and one purchase, she suggested that we head for the pubs. Unfortunately, we proceeded to drink from lunchtime onwards and by teatime we were pretty slaughtered. Sat in the Hogs Head pub on Canal Street, Samantha said that she had wondered what it would be like to kiss me. So, fuelled by a few vodkas, I just went for it, and we must have kissed in there for quite some time. And that was the start of my last ever (non-platonic) relationship with a woman.

Samantha and I headed back to Blackpool in the middle of the evening by train and our behaviour on the train journey was shocking, to the extent that I'm surprised we weren't thrown off. Back in Blackpool, we stopped in a couple more pubs, where this carried on until we were warned about our amorous behaviour, and finally got a cab back to my house, where Darren, his brother, Shaun, and sister-in-law, Ruth, were sat chatting. We ended up having a couple of joints before Samantha headed off home and I was left wondering what the hell had happened.

The next morning, a Saturday, I contacted Samantha and we agreed that it all just shouldn't have happened. But, later that week, we both had to travel down south to Crawley where we had some meetings in Head Office, and this involved an overnight stay. We weren't even drunk this time, but we'd agreed to stay in the same bed together, at her suggestion. So, we just had a cuddle and lay there spooning for a while. But, before I knew it, things were starting to happen (I think I already knew we wouldn't just be able to cuddle and fall asleep) so I just went with the flow. Surprisingly, it was actually really nice, although I was a bit taken aback. I didn't complain though.

That next morning was the first of numerous occasions where we ended up making love, and probably marked the start of our affair. Most days after that, we were finding excuses to disappear off somewhere and have some fun.

We did take some pretty silly risks when it came to meeting up. In fact, we were pretty appalling when I think back.

This relationship carried on for a good few months, past my departure from the job in Fleetwood and into my new role in one of Her Majesty's Prisons. Even in my new job at the prison, Samantha would come up and spend the night in my bed when I occasionally stayed in a B & B there (it was quite a drive from home, and some nights I just couldn't face sitting in traffic for hours on end).

Eventually, working away got to be too much, although we saw each other at weekends for a while and at least once a week when I was away. Once Samantha had left Simon and moved to her sisters, we sort of agreed that we should call it off, as it all seemed to be getting a bit too serious and far too scary. I then decided I would make one last attempt to get me and Darren sorted out, if that was at all possible.

It must have been in about May 2003, after things had died down, when Samantha sent me a text asking if she could meet me. So, I took the dog Jenna out for a walk to the Solarium Park on the promenade in Blackpool and met her there. Oddly, although she hadn't given me any clues, I knew exactly what this was going to be about before I met her, and my heart was racing when she finally pulled up in her car and walked towards me.

After a brief hug and a peck on the cheek, we started to walk over to the promenade. Samantha pulled a paper packet out of her bag, put it in the nearest bin and then she told me – she was pregnant, about twelve weeks at that stage. The packet she had put in the bin was the pregnancy test and its box. I think I must have gone into a silence for a period of time, but we had an amicable and sensible discussion about it. I asked what she wanted to do and said that I would love her to have the child. However, she said that, from her perspective, she wouldn't unless I started a life with her and we brought up the child together. This was something I just wasn't prepared to do. It wasn't about the fact that I would have to leave Darren; it was that I would have to pretend to be straight, and at least try to commit myself to a woman for the rest of my life. There was no way on this earth that was ever going to work; I knew myself all too well and I couldn't and wouldn't keep up that sort of pretence. I'd end up hating her and probably her me as well. Plus, if the baby was born, I'd potentially be ruining its life as well.

We agreed at the end of the walk that I would go round to her house the following day and talk some more. We said we would try and resolve the situation together, i.e. that we'd arrange for her to have an abortion if there were no other options. I was totally gutted at this prospect, but I knew there was no other choice for either of us. The whole relationship had really been foolish on my part and I expect this was the price I had to pay for it.

That night, all I did back indoors was think about what might happen in the future if tried to go straight for a while. The lying, deceit and my own need for sex with men would ruin it altogether, and I just wouldn't be able to live with the guilt. I couldn't think of any other way to keep the baby; she was pretty clear that I would need to be in a relationship with her if she were to continue with the pregnancy and wouldn't entertain the idea of having the baby and handing it to me to raise without her.

So, the next day, once with Samantha, we chatted and

agreed what we would do. I made the calls and we booked her into a clinic in Manchester for a day in the following week. We both booked the day off work, although I had to lie to Darren and say I was going to Strangeways Prison in Manchester for a meeting, as I wouldn't be leaving the house until later in the morning than usual.

It was a horrendous, gut-wrenching day. After a very quiet drive to Manchester, we parked at the clinic and both went in. Samantha was given a pill to take, and then shortly afterwards, she was taken in for the procedure to terminate the pregnancy. I was sat outside in the car while most of this was going on and was having some horrible thoughts – wondering if it was a boy or a girl, wondering if it felt any pain – and just feeling terribly guilty about the whole thing. I had been wondering if there was anything I could do to stop the whole thing, but it was too late for any of that. What felt like my sole chance of fatherhood was ruined and I had no idea if I would ever have that chance again.

I waited for what seemed like an eternity for Samantha to come out of there and she was quite upset, although she said she felt okay physically. We hardly spoke again on the way home and I took her back to her place, where she planned to go to bed. And that was that – no baby, no affair, just back to a mundane but comfortably convenient life with Darren.

For quite some time after that day, life was almost always clouded by the fact that I had been so close to having a family of my own, or at least a child, but it hadn't happened. I had started to wonder at that point if there was anything else I could do to have a child or if there would be someone who might want to do it for me. But, at that stage, I didn't take it any further. It didn't even seem like a real possibility and I don't think I would have wanted to go through that while I was in the relationship I was in. It would have been pointless and tied me down to a fairly unhappy existence in a life which really didn't suit me at all.

Moving On

In March 2005, after being self-employed for about two years, I took a part-time contracting role with an organisation just outside of Edinburgh. I was then spreading my days between Scotland and another role with a central government department with bases in London, Liverpool and Nottingham, and I was still with Darren.

That new role brought about some major changes for me: within a couple of months, Darren and I had eventually parted company and I was spending more and more time in Scotland. I met Marc shortly after that and was starting a whole new life for myself. It was all pretty scary, but I threw myself into it headlong.

Marc was three years older than me. In fact, it was exactly three years, as we both share the same birthday of 9 August, something we both found highly amusing. He hadn't been in a long-term relationship since he moved from his home town of Aberdeen to Edinburgh a few years earlier. He'd been honest with me about his enjoyment of living his life as a single man since then, but he had been clear about wanting to make a go of things with me, even after only knowing each other for a couple of weeks.

I did have some doubts about whether things would work out with us over the longer term. Our pasts had been very different; he had been married previously until his mid-twenties, and as a result had a 12-year-old daughter, Rebecca, who lived with her mum in Aberdeen. I found this quite off-putting initially, which I think was mainly down to the fact that he would be away quite a bit, and it was something I just wasn't used to.

Having said that, I agreed to make a go of things, but first had to have a conversation with Marc about his commitment to making our relationship work. It was during that conversation that Marc said that he loved me, and that he didn't want anyone else in his life but me. So, that was that, I really had no choice but to believe him, and I felt the same way about him.

It was probably about only a month after we first got together that Marc asked if we could get our own place in Edinburgh, so on 15 June 2005, we moved into Lynedoch Place in the West End, a lovely old Georgian terrace, where we had the basement flat with two bedrooms. I had been temporarily living in a rented flat in Stockbridge in Edinburgh, though Marc had been there with me most nights since we met. He had been living in a shared flat in the New Town, and I think he had had enough of the issues that sharing with complete strangers can bring.

Marc had also just decided to make another real change in his life – to leave his full-time, well-paid retail management job, and study at university to get a degree which would help him move into a totally different line of work in a public service role. This also meant that he would be worse off for the following three years, although he did get a part-time role working in a call centre for one of the local banks. However, he had asked me, when we were about to move in together, if I would help him out financially, so I reluctantly agreed to do so, paying for all the food bills in return for him doing the cleaning. I'm not sure I got the better end of the deal with that one – we both had very healthy appetites, yet the amount of cleaning required for a small two-bedroomed flat is fairly limited ...

The first year or so together brought all the fun and enjoyment you would expect in any positive relationship. We had our trips away around the UK, spent some time in Aberdeen and I met his daughter, which was a really enjoyable experience. We also started to make plans together for the future, buying flats and houses for investments.

We did have some rocky times during that year; getting used to each other's ways, habits, preferences and expectations can sometimes be difficult, but we managed to survive and at the end of that year, we moved again, this time into a massive detached bungalow on Queensferry Road, just on the way out of town. This really was a lovely family home, and for the most part, life improved there – we had a garden, garage, and lots of space to move around in, as well as plenty of rooms to use to avoid each other if we needed a bit of private space.

Making a Start

By early 2007, I had started to think more and more about the prospect of becoming a dad. It had never really left my mind since the episode with Samantha and in some respects I had seen what it might be like, having spent time with Marc and his daughter when she visited us, which really wasn't regularly enough.

By this time, I had managed to give some thought to my life and what I wanted, and had thoroughly assessed the situation I was in; I was well off financially in most respects, I was earning good money, had a few investment properties to help with my distant retirement, and I had a partner who had told me on a number of occasions that I was enough for him in all respects, that he loved me and wanted to spend his life with me. It was this latter point that was most important to me – the money was obviously going to be a necessity, but far more important to me was having the love, support and commitment of someone who I loved equally. So, taking all of this into account, I built up the courage to try and get what it was that I wanted – a child and family of my own.

One night, when Marc and I were sat in our lounge in Queensferry Road, I said to him that having a child was something I wanted us to do. It felt like an odd thing to say, but I meant it. I knew, being a gay man, it wasn't going to be the easiest thing in the world to achieve, but I was prepared to give it a go. By this time, I was starting to think that if I didn't start now I never would.

I can't remember the exact detail of the conversations we had, but I remember it was mentioned briefly a few times until one Sunday night when we were sitting chatting in the bath, and Marc agreed that, if it was something I really wanted, he would support me and we could go ahead with it.

11

He also said that it wouldn't be too bad having a little nipper running around, so that was that – I was over the moon about the fact that I was going to get this chance to at least try to be a father, and that I would have the support of my partner in doing it.

I wanted to do this for the right reasons, because I wanted a child to love and look after, and that was all there was to it. There was no other reasoning. I have always had a lot of love to give, and I've not really had the opportunity to do it with the choices I have made in life and the people I have shared it with. If I'm honest with myself, I suppose this was something I would have wanted to do whether I was in a relationship or not, although I would never have actually done it alone: too much stress, anxiety and lots of issues about intentionally becoming a single parent as a single gay man, which I would have found too difficult to deal with. I also certainly wouldn't have even started the process if there had been any doubts in either mine or Marc's minds. This was something that needed 100% commitment from both of us. As long as I was financially secure and continued to have this need and Marc's love, honesty and support, then I wanted to make it happen. Having a partner as support would be great and we would be like our own little family. The fact that I didn't have a woman to have a baby for me was irrelevant in terms of wanting to be a dad. For me, that was just an obstacle we would have to overcome.

At that time, I would regularly spend weekends in Blackpool with Darren when Marc was away with his daughter in Aberdeen. My social circle of friends was in Blackpool, and I didn't want to keep spending weekends alone in Edinburgh. The weekend after Marc had indicated he would be happy to go ahead and try to have a child, Darren had invited my parents over for dinner on the Saturday evening. So, full of excitement, I told them about my plans, when Darren was out of the room. I can still recall the look on their faces: surprise, confusion and shock. There seemed to be a glint of positivity from my mum, though Dad was probably pretty taken aback by the prospect of it all. Still, I knew that would change.

Before I returned to Edinburgh the next day, I called in at their house to say goodbye again as I wanted to have a more open conversation about the whole thing. I have to say, it didn't go as well as expected with my dad. He had said to me that a child needs a mother, which I took to mean that he didn't think I should do this at all. I suppose I should have expected this to a certain extent, as my parents are traditional people, Catholic, and used to a life where 'normal' things happened. I wasn't deterred at all though.

For the previous few weeks, I'd been doing a lot of research on the internet about surrogacy. I'd found a number of organisations in the UK who could potentially help, but when I called or emailed them, they told me that they would only provide support for heterosexual couples and definitely not for gay men.

I then approached Pink Parents, a UK organisation that supports gay parents, to see if they could help and they told me that if I joined, they might be able to put me in touch with a gay woman who wants to enter into a joint parenting arrangement. This really didn't do it for me; I wanted a child that I could bring up with Marc, not a half share of one with all the other complications that could go with it. What if we ended up not getting on? Or what if she decided to move away, or we didn't get on with her partner, or we disagreed about names, or schools, or holidays, or custody? It just all seemed far too risky and complicated for me.

I think it was Pink Parents who told me about an organisation called Man-Not-Included, who they thought might be able to do something. The company's name gave me the impression that they might not have been the most professional set up, but I looked them up on the internet and found a link to one of their websites, The Fertility Group, containing information about their surrogacy introduction service. It sounded professional enough, so I dropped them a brief enquiry.

I got a pretty quick response, which confirmed that they would help a gay couple with a surrogacy process. We then exchanged a few emails which helped me to get a better idea about the whole thing. Soon enough, I agreed to call them so I could talk it all through a bit better, which is what I did. I spoke to a chap called John Gonzalez, but was on the phone to him for probably just a few minutes. My first impressions of him were mixed; he seemed okay, but was pretty vague about the whole thing.

By this time, I had managed to find out about the costs that were going to be involved. The biggest expense was the fee payable to the fertility group; it was a hell of a lot of money and coupled with the amount I would need to pay for IVF treatment, an egg donor, the surrogacy fee and travel to the fertility clinic in Cyprus, it was all going to cost me about £30,000, or so I thought.

I was earning a substantial amount of money at this time. I was on a £450 per day fee, which basically meant that I could probably pay for it all out of just over three months' income, so although the cost was astronomically high, I wasn't particularly worried about it. I knew at the start that I would be the one paying for all of this; at the time, Marc was a student doing his degree at Queen Margaret in Edinburgh and he was still working part-time at the bank, so there was no chance of a penny coming from his wallet, but that didn't bother me. This was my dream, albeit a dream I wanted to share with Marc, and if it ever came to anything, it would be my child genetically, so it felt right that I was paying for this part of the process. However, I always wanted to make sure it felt like the child was both of ours, in terms of parental responsibility.

As soon as I felt I knew enough about the whole process, and after getting some form of a 'yes' from Marc, I arranged a meeting with John Gonzalez and set the ball rolling. We flew down to Luton in March 2007, hired a car from the airport and drove to their offices, which seemed to be in the middle of nowhere. It was at this time that I started to have some reservations about John. When we got to the offices, there was an old Lotus sports car parked outside with the registration plate 'SPERM1', which I guessed would have been his. Tacky as hell! That put both me and Marc off for a start, but anyhow, we went in to meet the guy.

The office seemed like a fairly professional setup; there were two or three girls working in there and we were taken to a small office at the end of the building where we sat and waited for John. He was a chubby, cheesy looking guy with a London accent, smartly dressed and a bit of a know-it-all. Our chat with him wasn't really what I expected; he asked some questions about us, our lifestyle, past histories and families and wrote it all down while we were chatting. He talked us through the process very briefly again and basically said that if we wanted to go ahead, I just needed to give him a call and we could go for it. I had to ask about the financial side of the process, and John explained that, if we wanted to go ahead, we would pay an initial, up-front payment of £6,000 to his company, and then eight further payments of £1,500 each. Gulp! That meant even before we knew a baby would be on the way, it would be costing us £18,000 in total, and that didn't include the payments to a surrogate, or indeed for the IVF treatment.

Marc and I chatted for a while after we'd met John. Neither of us was overly impressed, but I said I wanted to go ahead as there was nobody else in the UK who could help. I had looked into going to the States to do it, and there was a really high success rate there, but I just wasn't comfortable about it all happening so far away from me in a strange land. I needed some element of control and involvement in the process and I wouldn't get it if it was all happening thousands of miles away.

It wasn't until June 2007 that I eventually made my first payment to the fertility group and once it arrived with them, the process started, albeit at a frustratingly slow pace.

Our First Meeting

John initially arranged for us to meet with three potential surrogates down in London, in the city centre, so I booked flights for us to go down there. It was a midweek day, so it cost me a day off work, which I didn't mind at the time.

The day we were due to fly down there, I'd called John to confirm everything was okay, but just couldn't get hold of him. This made me panic a bit; we were travelling all that way and we didn't know what the proper arrangements were or anything, or the details of who we were meeting. After hours of not being able to get hold of him, I finally lost it and had a real good rant at whoever was answering the phone at the other end. This prompted her at least to get him to call me, which he did after a few minutes. I felt quite guilty afterwards, as it was just a call-centre girl I had spoken to as John had outsourced his company's call answering service. But at least I got to speak to him. It was at that stage that we were told we just had two people to meet the next day. That prompted a feeling of doom about the next day even before it had started.

Once we got to London and to the hotel, a girl called Emma who worked with John, called us to say that one of the women had backed out for some reason, which then meant we had travelled all that way to meet just one (my feelings of doom were becoming a reality!). I had the thought going through my mind that the last one was going to back out as well, and we would have travelled all of that way for nothing. I was trying my best not to worry, but I couldn't help it.

That night, we went out for a couple of beers around Soho and had a nice enough time, and the next morning we were ready to go and meet a woman called Karen. We were due to meet her with John at 11.00 a.m. at some place in the city when, lo and behold, another call came from Emma – Karen wasn't well and wasn't sure she could make it.

I could have killed her if she had been there in person, and I think she probably guessed that from the tone of my voice and my language. Thankfully, we managed to sort something out at least and John agreed to collect Karen and take her to Stansted Airport where we would meet them at a hotel. It all didn't bode well at all.

We had been sitting in the hotel lounge for what seemed like hours. I didn't have a clue what to expect; I'd never met someone wanting to act as a surrogate before and really didn't know whether she would be a sort of real maternal woman, bouncy, bubbly and full of life, or someone who was doing this for financial reasons and was cold and uncaring.

When they turned up an hour late, I couldn't have been more disappointed. Karen was forty-two, miserable looking and didn't look like she was interested in this at all, so some of my earlier thoughts and hopes about her were totally off the mark. She brought her young daughter along, who was just a toddler, and we found that odd, but we had to make a go of the meeting to see how it would go.

John went off to get us a coffee from the hotel bar, so we tried chatting to Karen and it was like talking to a very cold and grey brick wall. She had no interest in us at all, and now I can't remember much of anything about her. I just remember asking her one question and the answer put us off her altogether. One of the principles I wanted to stick to throughout this whole process was that of openness and honesty, as well as making sure whoever did it had their own support. So, I asked her what her partner thought about her going through the surrogacy process, to which she replied, 'Oh, he doesn't know. It's nothing to do with him.' That was the end of that for me.

The meeting was a total waste of time as far as I was

concerned. I couldn't imagine having to go through such a process with a woman I just knew we wouldn't get on with, let alone trust. Plus, she was over forty and would have had a minimal chance of success with IVF treatment. She would just have been too big a risk.

Once we had all finished chatting, we asked for a private moment with John and told him how we felt. We then said goodbye to Karen and her daughter, and went on our way back to the airport and off home. I tried speaking to Marc about it all on the way home as I was feeling quite dismayed and down about this experience, but I sensed a lot of discomfort from him. He obviously didn't want to talk about it at all, so it was a very quiet journey all the way back to the front door. At this point, I was seriously thinking this had all been a set-up. Was Karen actually a real person? Was she one of John's friends called in to make it look like a real process? And was John playing on our desire to have a child, knowing that we would go along with whatever was organised just so we felt he and his company were authentic? I never got to find out.

But, the next day, I called John to see where we would go next. He said he would now start looking for other potential surrogates who could work with us, and would come back to us as soon as possible. So, it was simply a case of waiting. I did explain to him that we wanted to meet people who were probably the opposite of Karen – at least able to hold a decent conversation and embarking on this process for the right reasons, with their own support network – but I was starting to feel like that was maybe asking a bit too much.

Katie

It was a while before we were offered the chance of another meeting. This time it was with someone called Katie Jones; she was about twenty-five and married with two children of her own. We did think that was a bit young, but I suppose that this was from the perspective of the age gap between us and her; I worried about my ability to relate as well to someone at that age. However, I told John we'd be happy to meet her and another meeting was arranged. It was in London yet again and I dreaded the prospect of the travel down there, as well as having to tell Marc about it. But I eventually did and we went to the offices of an accountant in Old Street, after a wander round the city, to meet them one Saturday.

Katie and Will were there before us. John and Emma met us there in reception, said a quick hello and took us straight into a meeting room to meet Katie and Will. They did actually seem like a nice couple and we had a fairly open chat; at least this time we were able to have a decent two-way conversation. They were asking us what we did for a living and about Rebecca, Marc's daughter, and why we wanted children. That part of it came from me, as would always be the case, but it was a positive meeting and when it ended, I was feeling pretty optimistic about it all. Marc seemed a bit more interested this time as well, which made me feel better too. I was feeling relieved that he had been able to take part in the conversation, and that he seemed quite relaxed talking about himself and Rebecca. Maybe things were looking up after all.

When we got home, I called John to let him know that we would be happy to work with Katie. It seemed like she had her head screwed on and that she knew what she was doing.

When I spoke to John, I explained to him that we would like to be able to get to know Katie outside of meetings with him, so I asked if he would be open to us exchanging numbers so that we could give her a call and arrange to meet again. It took a couple of days, but we eventually got hold of her number and we called her one night after work. Again, we had a good chat and she was happy for us to go down to Boston in Lincolnshire to meet them.

It wasn't too long a wait before we met her and Will in a pub in Boston for lunch. It was actually a good meeting, although there was a six-hour drive either side of it. We were in the Audi TT, so at least we were able to go pretty quickly; well, as quickly as you can on the A1 at the weekend.

When we were there, we got on to the subject of John and his ways. Katie thought he seemed like a bit of a dodgy guy and it turned out that she didn't know much, if anything, about the whole process between entering into an agreement and the actual birth. It turned out that Katie had actually only volunteered to be an egg donor through John's company, not a surrogate, but they had asked her if she would consider surrogacy and she said she would. So, we suggested that she called John to get an idea of what was involved and how it would be managed. She then started to talk about the prospect of only involving him until there was a confirmed pregnancy, so that he couldn't have any control over any of the rest of it. She came across as quite mistrusting of him and sadly this was due to get worse.

After a few days, I spoke to Katie again and it felt like her mood about the whole process had changed somewhat. She started talking about the financial side of the deal and the fact that she was the one who really wasn't getting much out of it; we were getting a child, John would get quite a lot of money, but the amount she was due to get was minimal compared to what she had to go through. Yet again, she brought up the possibility of doing this without John, but we never reached any agreement. She also told me that she had done some research about John online and had found all sorts of negative stories about him, the sperm-bank service he had offered and that other organisations had warned her to steer well clear of him.

At the end of the conversation, I suggested that if she felt the need, she should speak to John about all of the financial arrangements, as it wasn't something I felt I should be getting involved in at that stage. Very shortly after that, I was sat at work and received an email from John asking me to get in touch as soon as I could. I called him and he had the biggest rant at me that anyone has ever had. He basically said we were never to get in touch with Katie again, that we have ruined the whole process and that we could no longer work with her. He also said that if we insisted on carrying on changing 'the process', whatever that might be, then he would not be able to continue working with us. That left me in pieces, but I gave him as good as I got. For me, meeting Katie was about trying to form some sort of relationship so we could trust her enough to hand the baby over after the birth. I wouldn't go through the process if I couldn't do that.

That night was the first night that I became very upset about the whole thing; I felt that it was never going to work, that John was just a total idiot and that he didn't have a clue how to manage this whole thing at all. He just seemed so inefficient that I really expected it all to go tits-up. So, after a couple of glasses of wine, I ended up in tears at home, feeling pretty despondent. At least that night I felt like I did get some support from Marc, however uncomfortable he was starting to appear to be about the whole thing.

I didn't call Katie again; I just didn't see the point. I had no real idea what she had said to John or what he had said to her, or even why he had pulled the plug on the whole thing. Plus, I don't expect that surrogacy is something you can really persuade a total stranger to do, especially if they have a major issue with it, or even any element of it. So, onwards we went, yet again, with no idea of whether this was ever going to happen.

Denise

The next step again was for us to meet someone else. This time, we were invited down to Uxbridge to meet John, Emma and someone called Denise. Seemingly, she had been through the surrogacy process already up to the IVF stage, although it hadn't worked. She had a supportive partner, a son and a step-daughter, and totally understood what was involved. That gave me some reassurance, although we weren't overly enthralled by the idea of meeting John again. I was feeling positive about her, though, especially as she had the same birthday as me and Marc – 9 August.

We travelled down again on a Saturday, flying to Heathrow and then getting the train to Uxbridge, where we found our way to the offices. It now seemed that they were based in serviced office accommodation rather than in their own building that we visited before on the opposite side of London. I didn't ask why; I thought I was probably better off not knowing.

We saw some people waiting outside the building as it was locked, but then John came down to find us and let us in. It turned out that the other people were Denise, her partner and Denise's son. We were all ushered up to a meeting room, John did the introductions and we started the usual chats. Denise seemed nice enough, a bit older than Katie and quite level headed. We had the usual chat about reasons for doing it and home life, and then John proceeded to ask Denise to show us her pictures of their cat. It was the most bizarre thing in the world to have done and it just stopped the conversation dead. He is such a weird bloke. Maybe he just thought gay men automatically liked cats, so we would be impressed. He was wrong – neither of us was impressed at all and we must have looked quite uncomfortable (though I do admit to having owned a few cats in my time).

Marc had been very quiet during this meeting again and I was beginning to get the impression that he didn't want to be part of it, but he didn't say anything to suggest that. Anyhow, by the end of the forty-minute chat, I felt fairly comfortable with Denise, but these things are so difficult; how on earth, in such a short space of time, can you assess whether someone can carry a child for you and whether they would be prepared to hand it over? I suppose the short answer is that you can't; all you can do is go with your gut instinct (which can quite frequently be very, very wrong, as I was to find out later on), coupled with a tendency to try and be positive, as you don't want to ruin your chances of finding anyone at all by turning someone down who seems to be okay on the face of it. Marc and I chatted afterwards about Denise, and he said he was happy for us to go forward again and see what happened. I also double-checked that he was still happy overall for us to be doing this, with the potential end result of a child, and he confirmed he was. Sometimes when we talked about this whole process, Marc seemed quite distant about it, and even though he said the right things most of the time, I had started to get the impression he wasn't overly excited by the prospect of becoming a dad again.

Anyhow, here we went again. I told John on the following Monday that we'd be happy to go with Denise and he quickly passed on contact details so that we could chat and get to know her a bit, which surprised me, bearing in mind what had happened with Katie. As usual, it was me rather than Marc who was doing the chatting, and Denise and I spoke a few times, just in general terms about life and work.

It wasn't too long before John actually arranged for us to go to Harley Street for a consultation and to start the whole process in terms of IVF treatment. That was as far as I knew anyway. So, yet again, we travelled down there and went into a clinic-type place, where we met Denise and her step-daughter.

Denise, Marc and I had to go into a meeting with the consultant so that he could take some details: Denise's previous medical history, my personal statistics and also what we would be looking for in an egg donor. Denise also had to go in for a scan to check that all was well with her womb. It all seemed straightforward enough, but I did get the impression that the clinic wasn't such a reputable place. We were down in the basement of an enormous building; it was damp, dark and altogether drab. There were also some pretty odd-looking characters about.

Sadly Denise's scan showed that she had some sort of cyst in her ovary and the consultant said that we would need to wait for that to go away before any IVF treatment could start. It didn't seem to be too much of a problem though and once home, Denise and I carried on chatting every now and again over the phone for a while.

Jailing John

One day, during this time, I went online to read the *Daily Mail* and there it was – John Gonzalez's picture with a headline that read, 'Fertility 'crusader' unmasked as a fraudster who stole £200,000.' On 9 April 2008, John was sent to prison for sixteen months for effectively spending the money that investors had put into one of his other companies – mannotincluded.com! He was also banned from being a company director for five years. Yet again, panic set in. What the hell were we supposed to do now? If John had been jailed then surely that sent this whole thing down the pan.

On the off-chance that she could tell me at least something, I called Emma to a) tell her how gutted I was to read about this in the paper without having been told by her first and b) find out if there was any chance this thing was going to come off. Emma did apologise and told me that John was now nothing at all to do with her or the company, and that she would be running things from now on. I wasn't altogether happy, but what else could I do but trust her? So, on we carried. I had a brief chat with Denise about it and she didn't seem too disturbed at all, which was a relief.

Out of the blue, a few weeks after the scan, Emma called me to let me know that Denise and her partner had separated temporarily, and that Denise was now staying in Wales for a while, so the whole process would be put on hold. My hopes were dashed yet again. I think I knew at this point that it wasn't going to work out with Denise. It sounded bizarre that 'they had separated temporarily'; surely couples never know if these things are going to be temporary or not?

Anyway, as luck would have it, a few weeks later, she was back home with her partner and we were told that it was all going to go ahead again, and then another few days went by before I was told that it was off again. This time, her partner had told her that he didn't want her to go through with the surrogacy, so that was that. Back to square one yet again.

By now, I was wondering what to do, so I got in touch with a company in the States again to talk about starting the whole process. The prospect of spending a whole load more money was not exciting me at all, but I felt like I was at least doing something. They sent me registration forms and quite a lot of literature which I pondered over for a while, but I just wasn't inspired.

Jemma

In the summer of 2008, Emma contacted me again to say that they had now found someone else who might be able to act as surrogate for us. This time it was someone called Jemma Paris (the name just didn't sound right). She had seven (yes, seven!) children of her own and lived in Glamorgan in Wales. Seemingly, she was good friends with someone who was going through surrogacy, which at least was half the battle, though this never came up in conversation with her throughout the time we were in touch.

So, yet again, we agreed to meet. With all the previous history of us travelling to London and the expense I had incurred so far for seemingly no reason at all, I said to Emma that Jemma would need to come up to Edinburgh for us to meet her. Emma, however, had originally thought that Glamorgan was somewhere near us in Scotland, which didn't surprise me given her obvious lack of intelligence. Financially, travelling south wouldn't have been an issue for me. But, the prospect of having to tell Marc we were heading south again wasn't a good one and as a matter of principle, I wanted someone else to be making the effort. So, it was arranged; Emma would bring Jemma and her sister up to Edinburgh and we would all meet at the airport one lunchtime.

Jemma wasn't what I expected at all. This is going to sound really snobby, but she came across as really common; not down to earth or working class, just common. However, she could at least hold a conversation and her sister seemed nice. Jemma was in her mid-to-late thirties with a tarty (or too young; I couldn't work out which) dress sense and a very odd hairstyle with bits going off in all directions, and some strange colours, but she seemed enthusiastic enough.

So, yet again, we said yes. We must have been gluttons for punishment.

Jemma was actually very good at keeping in touch; she called and chatted quite a few times and we did have a good laugh. She was all for telling her mates about the surrogacy process and her sister was seemingly quite supportive. Her sister was pregnant at this time, but it was her own child.

Then it all started to go pear-shaped again ...

Jemma was due to go to London for a scan, to check that everything internally was in the right place. On the day she was due to go, however, she just cut all contact. Neither I nor Emma could get hold of her; she wasn't answering her phone or text messages and we didn't have a clue what was going on. This silence lasted a few days, until she finally got in touch with Emma to say that her son had been in a car accident in Essex. He had seemingly been knocked over in the street and was in hospital with his legs bandaged and some apparently quite serious damage. So, she had dropped everything to get over to Essex (I have no idea why, but he lived with his aunty over there) and had spent days by his bed in hospital. She said that she didn't want to talk to anyone until she knew he was going to be okay.

Jemma and I were back in touch after a while and she explained everything to me, but I just didn't believe it. It all seemed to be quite far-fetched and unbelievable, and I got the strong impression that yet again, this was not going to work out. At this stage in the whole process, the egg donor had been chosen and booked, and all was planned for the treatment to create the embryos to take place in November 2008. So, it was vital that Jemma was committed to seeing it all through.

I was obliged to send money to Jemma to pay for the medication she would need at the start of the process; this was the medication which would stop her having periods and keep the lining of her womb intact so that the embryos would have something to stick to once they were implanted. I think I must have sent her about £500 in total, including enough for the trip to London for her scan. She had to go back to London in October for another scan so that the consultants could work out exactly the right time for the embryo transfer, and this was when it finally went tits-up. On the day Jemma was due to go, she told me she had no money and couldn't afford the train ticket. I just knew then that she was taking the piss. According to her, she had been overdrawn and the money I had already sent her had been swallowed up, so she just couldn't get a ticket.

I plainly refused to send any more cash, knowing that this wasn't going to work out. So, that was that – it was all over yet again. I did send Jemma a couple of nasty text messages, just to make myself feel better, but it didn't really help. She had pocketed all of the cash she had been sent and there was no remorse, or repayment, whatsoever. I thought it wise to delete her details from my phone, as otherwise I would have carried on sending more messages and I thought I was better than that.

My Trip to Cyprus

We now had a nightmare situation on our hands; the egg donor was halfway through her treatment and there was no way that she could be told to hang on. Emma called me to say that I was going to have to go out to Cyprus, deposit some semen there and they would make the embryos, which would then be frozen and implanted when we had a surrogate ready for them.

I booked my trip half-heartedly. This was supposed to be a great moment, but it was just horrendous – a return trip to Cyprus by myself (Marc didn't want to come) with no prospect of a baby being born because of it. It was very depressing indeed. On Friday 7 November 2008, I drove to Manchester Airport to catch my flight, feeling very alone, which made me feel worse. So, I sat in the airport lounge with a few hours to kill and managed to have a few glasses of wine before getting on the plane. I did manage to have a chat with Kim, my good friend and colleague from my first ever consultancy contract, and we made light of the situation, which helped to pass some of the time until I boarded my plane.

It was a long and boring journey, and I had even more wine on the plane, just because I could. When I eventually got off in Cyprus, I proceeded to have a humorous bartering session with a taxi driver so I could get a cheap trip to my hotel, which was about forty-five minutes away from the airport. But I think I still ended up paying about €60 – extortionate.

The hotel felt like a tourist trap, with people milling about with red chests and faces and flip-flops. I just went to my room, checked out the (dark) view and then went outside to find a shop and buy some fags and food. I was on a real downer by this point. What was supposed to be one of the most exciting experiences of my life was, at this stage, one of the most depressing things I had ever been through. It just felt all wrong and had become such a lonely experience.

After a brief walk around the local area and a few smokes, I headed back to my room and put the telly on; I couldn't find one English channel and just had to leave the thing on for some background noise. I tried calling some friends but got no response. I called Marc and we spoke briefly, but about nothing of any significance. So, there I was, sat in my room, very alone and feeling very sorry for myself. I couldn't even indulge in any type of light relief; I had to abstain from any sexual activity for at least three days before going to the clinic in the morning to produce and hand over my semen. So, I went to sleep feeling quite frustrated and just wanting to get back home.

I woke up early the next morning and it was quite a nice day outside. The sun was shining and the view from my balcony was a pretty nice one; I could see the sea and lots of hotels about. I had a quick shower and then packed up my stuff, went downstairs and got the hotel staff to organise a taxi for me, which took me straight to the clinic.

The clinic itself was a nice-looking building, although it felt as though it was in a very run-down area of Limassol. I sat outside for a while, wondering if I would see the egg donor coming out, but I never did, unless of course it was the cleaning lady in overalls I saw leaving the building. So, in I went, asked for Lara and all she did was take me to a small room, without a word, and shut the door. It was quite comical. This room felt like a waiting room with a lockable door and contained a box full of sample jars and a TV and DVD player which didn't work, alongside which were some straight porn movies. Talk about uncomfortable and poorly equipped.

I was probably the least turned on I'd ever been when I

did the deed. However, I didn't take very long and managed to produce the goods, buckled myself up again and went back round to the reception desk, where my pot was handed to someone and I was asked to take a seat. I sat there not knowing where to look and feeling quite conscious that everyone there would know what I had just done. Weird!

Lara then came through to see me. I asked her if she had met the egg donor and she said she had – and that she was very beautiful, tall and slim. She then took me to meet the consultant, Dr Savvas, who sat me down and at least talked me through what would happen. I think it was the only decent conversation I had all the while I was in Cyprus. He explained that they had retrieved eleven eggs from the egg donor and that they would expect a really good chance of them working once we had a surrogate.

I was probably only in the clinic for about half an hour and I had quite a few hours to kill before I had to head back for my flight, so I wandered around aimlessly for half an hour or so. It was a lovely day, so I sat on the beach wall reading a magazine and people-watching for a while. It was a shame I hadn't brought any summer clothes, as I could have just sat on the beach in my shorts and caught some rays. I felt very out of place. I then decided to head into the town and find something to deal with my hunger, and I managed to find a breakfast place, which perked me up a bit. Then I had a walk around some shops, bought some undies in a department store and looked around for a baseball cap (I can never find a decent one) before finally deciding I should just head for the airport, so I got a taxi there with four hours to spare.

The airport was mobbed, but at least there was an open-air café where I could sit and smoke and drink numerous pints of Diet Coke to pass the time. It was a very long four hours; my mobile phone battery had died, so conversation was non-existent. I also made sure I spent the rest of my euros before finally getting on the plane and enduring the long flight back to Manchester.

It really had been a crap experience and I was just glad I didn't have to do it again. Or at least I hoped I didn't. From getting off the plane at about 7.00 p.m., I made a mad dash for the car and put my foot down all the way to Edinburgh. It must have been 11.30 p.m. by the time I was indoors and I was very glad to get there. Just to be able to sit down, have a drink and chill out was good. Also, to know that I hopefully wouldn't have to travel to Cyprus again in such a rush was a relief. But that still left me no further forward – embryos were being made and then frozen in Cyprus and I had nobody to act as a surrogate for me.

More Failure

Shortly before Christmas, Emma was in touch again to tell me about someone called Mandy: a girl in her later twenties who lived in Middlesex, had a child of her own and wanted to be a surrogate. By this time, I was running out of patience with these people and was starting to cringe at the prospect of meeting yet another one, with all the heartache that it could bring. Emma had arranged to go and meet Mandy first and the feedback from this was positive; seemingly Mandy was level headed, had a great family network around her, and was really keen to do this. So, Emma and I agreed that Mandy and I should talk over the phone before we arranged to meet, just to see how we got on.

On 10 December 2008, I called her for our first chat. As usual, she sounded nice: a strong, confident London accent, wanting to get into it for all the right reasons and she seemed to have her head screwed on. She lived beside her mum, had lots of support and felt good about her meeting with Emma. The next step was to go to London and meet her, which between the three of us we organised for a date towards the end of January 2009. It wasn't too far away and we agreed that we would chat again in the interim period.

I think we probably only chatted once more. Then, on 28 December 2008, I received a voicemail message from Emma on my mobile phone: Mandy could no longer participate in the process as she had fallen pregnant. Yet again, it was another blow. Seemingly, she was very upset as she really wanted to help us, but now she couldn't – yeah, yeah, yeah! Whatever! I found that all quite bizarre, as well as frustrating. How in God's name could someone who was apparently entering into a surrogacy process go ahead and get pregnant themselves? Yet again my overwhelming thought was 'is this ever going to happen?' So, there I was at square one again. At this stage I was thinking that I may as well just prepare myself for living at stage one for the next few years! It was all very disheartening to say the least.

The day I found out about Mandy's pregnancy, Rebecca arrived in Edinburgh and was there when I heard Emma's message. So, I couldn't really talk about the whole thing, but this was nothing new, with Marc just acting like it wasn't happening at all by this stage. Life just went on as normal, but I was feeling very down in the dumps.

Ana

Over the next couple of weeks, I spoke to Emma a few times and towards the middle of January, she came up with someone else. I can't quite believe I ever entertained the idea of putting myself through this again, but something inside me just kept me pushing ahead, no matter what the consequences were.

This time, it was a girl called Ana Karim who, it turned out, was part Egyptian as well as some other races. I had a chat with Ana over the phone and as usual, we got on just fine. She had two kids of her own, was a single mum and had just moved to Walsall, near Birmingham, having previously been living in London near to the rest of her family. Yet another meeting was arranged and on Sunday 15 February, Marc and I flew down to Heathrow for a meeting with Ana and Emma. Ana's mum was also there. I was dreading it.

I was quite taken aback by how stunning Ana was; although she sounded like a Londoner, she was obviously from a mixed race background and was very beautiful with striking features, long black hair and a petite build. We chatted a lot and her mum also joined in, and I felt pretty happy about the whole thing. I think I must have dropped all of my earlier standards by this point, so would have said yes to anyone, but Ana seemed far better than the rest for some reason.

Ana's mum tried to involve Marc in the conversation at one point; she asked him what his thoughts were about the whole thing, as he hadn't said a word so far. At this point, he did speak up, although really just to say that he was happy about it, adding a little summary of himself, and explaining about his daughter, so at least they were able to get to know him a little.

Leaving Heathrow that day, I sent a text to Emma saying that, yet again, we would be happy to go ahead with Ana. I also texted Ana to say that it had been great to meet her and that both of us thought she was lovely. Fingers, legs and everything else crossed for the umpteenth time! As usual, the conversation between Marc and me was limited and there was hardly any mention of surrogacy all the way home.

I have to say that I felt quite different about the whole thing this time. Ana and I chatted a few times over the phone and soon enough, she was going for the scans in London where they would assess her suitability and also work out the timing for the IVF to take place in Cyprus. Ana was always really positive; she said to me on our first phone call that she had made it her mission to have a baby for us. I had talked her through everything that had happened in the past, except for the problems with John Gonzalez, and she couldn't believe what had taken place.

So, she was in for her last scan on 20 March 2009 and on the 12 April, she flew to Cyprus. I think I was in a state of disbelief at that point. After suffering such lengthy delays, problems and emotional trauma, there we were with the potential of a baby actually being developed and born. She flew out to Cyprus with her cousin, and I paid for both of them, although it was only the flights, a two-night stay and a little money for some expenses. She let me know when she got there and kept in touch throughout her trip. The embryos were transferred on 13 April and when I got the message saying so I was as happy as Larry! It felt odd me being in the UK while this was going on, and I could happily blame Jemma for that one, but this was all really positive. This was as far into the process as we had ever got and now there were three embryos inside Ana, at least one of which could end up developing into a baby.

Once Ana was home, we spoke and she was feeling good about the whole thing. We chatted almost daily and she had been telling me that she did feel like she might be pregnant; she was getting a metallic taste in her mouth and was feeling a bit sick. Now all we had to do was wait for the first test to be done. I have to say, the waiting was awful. Pretty well known for my lack of patience, this was extremely frustrating for me.

Finally, after waiting for what seemed like an eternity, Ana took a test and phoned me. I was a bag of nerves by this point, about two weeks after the embryo transfer. When she called, I was calm, trying not to get too excited, so we said hello and then I listened. She told me that she had taken two tests; one showed a faint positive result and the second was negative. I really had no idea what this could have meant and Ana told me that you can get false negative results, but not false positive ones. So, she said she would take another test a couple of days later. I really wasn't sure how to feel at this stage. Was Ana just being positive for my sake? Or was she trying to let me down gently? The next time she phoned a couple of days later, she confirmed that the test results were negative. She had also started losing blood, which meant that the lining of her womb was coming away – no baby.

Although I was heavily disappointed, I took lots of positives from the experience; there was someone willing to go through this for us and the process could work (I knew from the outset that the success rate for IVF treatment wasn't a guaranteed 100%). But, we could now go for it again. Ana was as realistic about it as I was and said to me after she took the second test that she would be more than happy to go for it again. She even reiterated that she had made this her mission. So, it wasn't all bad. I was relieved that we had at least been able to get to this stage.

True to her word, Ana agreed to go through the process again pretty quickly. On 15 May, she started again with the initial injections and before I knew it, she was off to Cyprus yet again, although this time she went by herself. On 20 June

2009, three further embryos were transferred. This was quite a nail-biting time for me, as these were the last of the embryos being used. I hadn't realised, but each time they do a transfer they thaw more embryos than they need and only use the best ones. So, I had none left, although they still had some of my sperm out there.

This time, however, there was no metallic taste, no sickness, no nothing. I think I expected the worst and her pregnancy test confirmed it – there was to be no baby.

Ana was great about it as usual, and still was keen to carry on in the hope that she could carry a child for us. This meant a bit of a wait as we would have to find another egg donor, and she did want a break before we started again, so we agreed to keep in touch for a while until she was ready to go again. We thought it would probably start for the third time at some point in the autumn – September or October.

It was September when the whole process was about to start again. Emma and Ana were starting to sort out dates, although I hadn't been in touch with Ana as much as maybe I should. In mid-September, I spoke to Emma and she said that Ana was having doubts, as we hadn't been communicating with her. She also felt that I had blamed her for the last two transfers going wrong, which wasn't the case at all. I tried endlessly to call Ana and she did text a couple of times to say that her phone was on the blink. But, I never managed to speak to her again.

I had a long chat with Emma about this, but I did say that there was no point trying to get Ana to change her mind. This was too big a process to have to persuade someone to go through; it needed 100% commitment and obviously Ana didn't have that level of commitment any more. So, yet again, back to square one.

At this stage, I really wasn't sure about going through all the emotional turmoil again. Ana had been the only woman to have actually gone through with the process. My thinking was along the lines that if one in every five or six women would take the final step to IVF, then I would have a hell of a long time to wait until I found someone else to do it. I was despairing at this point and I didn't feel as if I could talk to Marc about it; the mere mention of the process brought on an uncomfortable silence from him. I didn't want to have to suffer that sort of mood again at that stage.

I also thought about contacting the organisation in the States again, but by this stage, I really couldn't afford it. My daily-rate work had finished in July 2008 and I had then been on a £50k salary for a charity in Edinburgh, but this job had also ended. Now I wasn't working and I didn't have any spare cash at all, let alone the £30,000 odd I'd need to be paying out to start the process in America.

So, I left it all in Emma's hands to keep pushing on. After what I had spent already, I took the view that it didn't make sense to just stop the whole thing. All the emotional turmoil would have been for no reason at all and the prospect of life without a child ever arriving just wasn't one I wanted to contemplate, although it was feeling fairly realistic at this point in time.

Kerry

Surprisingly, on 14 November, Emma yet again came up with someone else. This time, it was a girl called Kerry who lived in Glasgow, had three kids of her own and was married. We had never tried to go through it with anyone as close to home before, so maybe this would bring a different dimension to it.

The arrangement was to be that I called Kerry initially, so that we could speak on the phone and take it from there. At 1.00 p.m. on 14 November, I called Kerry and we had a good old chat. It turned out that she had offered to act as a surrogate for one of her aunts, but her aunt wanted total control over things such as diet and lifestyle, and Kerry couldn't live with that. She seemingly loved being pregnant, but didn't want any more children of her own. It was a positive chat. These first ones always were! During the phone call, she asked if she could see a picture of us and we agreed to go onto MSN Messenger so we could look at each other!

Kerry and I agreed to meet on 27 November in Glasgow. She was currently studying nursing and was off every Friday, so we agreed I would see her at Queen Street Station at 2.00 p.m. I was quite excited as it wasn't far to travel and it would be just the two of us. Emma said she didn't need to be there and Marc wasn't there either. So, it meant I could just be myself and we could have an open and honest chat about everything.

The morning I set off, I was feeling pretty good about it, probably just because at least something was happening again. I had seen the picture of Kerry online, so knew vaguely what she looked like, but I was still pretty unsure of what to expect when I got there. Finally, we met at 2.00 p.m., after I had wandered the streets for a while, and my first impressions were great. We ended up in the Buchanan

Galleries Shopping Centre having a coffee, and sat and chatted for about an hour. She was telling me about her home life and kids, and I was telling her all the reasons that I wanted to be a dad. We got on like a house on fire that day and I was very impressed. She was in her mid-twenties, 5 feet 5 inches and fairly slim, but a well-proportioned figure (not that her appearance has any bearing on the outcome of this whole thing).

Later that day, on the train on the way home, I received a text from her saying how nice she thought I was and how she would love to be able to help us have a baby. I said the same to her: that I thought she seemed really nice and that it would be great if she would be able to do it for us. So, yet again, I called Emma and told her my thoughts, and on we went.

By this time, in some respects, I was just going through the motions. I refused to get my hopes up about Kerry, even though I was feeling good about her. She had given me all the right messages and was very positive, but she had had a lot of complications with previous pregnancies, and I think she had had something like twelve pregnancies before, with only three of them being successful. Seemingly, she had some sort of blood disorder, which meant that at the six-week stage she would normally miscarry, although now she knew that if she took blood-thinning medication she would be okay. She also told me that when she had her last son, she was very ill after the birth, to the point where doctors thought she was going to die. Her sister was apparently distraught about it all, so she wasn't going to tell her about the surrogacy process until further down the line.

We again had to choose an egg donor for the whole process at this stage. This time, it was a Russian woman who had one child, was a florist and was married. We then arranged that Marc and I would go and meet Kerry on Friday 19 February at Ikea in Glasgow. There, we met Kerry, her youngest son and her daughter. Marc and I were there first and then Kerry and the kids arrived. As I expected, it was a fairly restrained and quiet meeting. Marc hardly said a word; he didn't ask Kerry anything and we generally just talked about Christmas and all the preparations involved in it. It was quite awkward actually, with Marc just sitting quietly, and there were a few embarrassing silences. To be honest, I was relieved when it was over.

Once we got home, I felt the need to text Kerry and told her that Marc thought she was great, but that he is always quiet when he meets new people. She said she felt as though he didn't like her as he hadn't said much at all, but I told her not to worry. By this stage, I was pretty certain that Marc had no real interest in this whole thing whatsoever. I kept trying to convince myself that he would take some sort of active role in the process, but it just never happened. I was beginning to face the realisation that the arrival of this child, if it was ever going to arrive, might turn me into the head of a single parent family.

The process with Kerry seemed to start pretty quickly after the meeting with Marc. We chatted a few times over the phone and she was as upbeat as ever about the whole thing. Her first injection had been on 10 February and her last scan before IVF was on 5 March. On 8 March, I picked Kerry and her mum up in Glasgow and drove them through to Edinburgh Airport, from where they started their trip to Cyprus. The embryo transfer took place on 9 March and they implanted three embryos, which was more than I expected, especially as Kerry had said that she only really wanted them to put one in. Anyway, the deed was done.

On 11 March, they returned home. It was my best pal Steve Barr's funeral in Blackpool that day, so it was all a major rush and a horrendously emotional day. I had to drive to Blackpool, go to see Steve's body and have a few quiet words, go to Steve's funeral, nip and see the family and then drive back home, following which I then had to head out to

Edinburgh Airport, pick Kerry and her mum up and then take them back through to Glasgow before driving home. Marc hadn't volunteered to help out at all. So, in addition to driving the best part of 600 miles during the day, I was shattered, pretty emotionally drained and feeling like I was alone in all of this. I eventually got to my bed at about 1.30 a.m., but I managed to stay as positive as my emotions would allow.

Well, that was that; another case of waiting. For someone with not a shred of patience, I was doing pretty well – in most respects anyway!

Just after the weekend, Kerry texted me and told me that she had been sick since the weekend. I wondered whether it could have been anything to do with morning sickness and I asked her what she thought it was. She said that it was not too early for morning sickness, but she didn't want to get my hopes up.

It's a Baby!

On 17 March at about 5.00 p.m., my phone rang – it was Kerry. Her first words were, 'Are you sitting down?' I knew straight away what she was going to tell me: she had taken a pregnancy test, as she had some left from when her youngest was born, and it was positive! Aaaaaarrrrggghhhhhh!!!!!!!!

She hadn't been due to take the test until the Saturday morning and said she would still do one then, but she knew when she was sick at the weekend that she was going to be pregnant. I was almost speechless! Oh my God! I didn't know what to say and ended up walking quickly around the house while she was talking to me. I was just so excited. I knew it was still very early days and things could still go wrong, but oh my God! A pregnancy!

I called Marc straight away, all excited and nervous, told him the news and was hoping against all odds that he was going to share my excitement. Sadly, the response I got was, 'Oh, jolly good.' That was it – jolly good! What sort of a bloody reaction was that? I think my feelings about him and his involvement in the whole thing were pretty correct – he had no interest in this at all and never would have as far as I could make out. I knew then that I was going to go through this pregnancy alone and I had no idea what to do about it.

I needed to stay upbeat and positive, so I called Mum straight away and told her; she was over the moon. Then I called Kerry back, as I had promised to once I'd told Marc, and I found myself lying to her, telling her that he was just as excited as me. It was a real shame and that, I think, really affected the state of our relationship badly at the time.

The next few weeks were full of anxiety. Kerry had morning sickness on and off, and there were all sorts of issues about getting her the right medication. When she was in Cyprus, she had told the consultant about the issues with her previous miscarriages and he had given her warfarin, a blood-thinning drug, and told her to take the injections along with aspirin. So, she was constantly taking something. But, Emma had been pretty dire in ensuring she had enough of the right pills and potions to take at the right time. Twice within the first eight weeks, Kerry ran out of pills, only for the next lot to be delivered the following day. It didn't make for a comfortable process at all. She also had to take medication for the first twelve weeks of the pregnancy to help her body realise she was pregnant, and then she would reduce the dosage until it ended. It did cost me a fortune, but at least we got them all in time.

Marc and I went to meet Kerry on 26 March in Ikea in Glasgow again. When Kerry arrived, she first showed us her stomach. It was black and blue from the warfarin injections and looked a real mess, as well as being slightly bigger than it looked the last time. Anyhow, this meeting was better than the last one; Marc did speak a few times and it was a lot more relaxed. We were there for about an hour and I was feeling good afterwards. It was all going well and I was over the moon.

As time went on, I was becoming more and more certain that a baby was going to appear at the end of it all. We managed to get a scan booked at the six-week stage, although Marc didn't want to come along. So, it was just Kerry and me. I met her at the Southern General Hospital in Glasgow, at 2.00 p.m., on 8 April, just into the second week of my new job with Edinburgh University. We had been joking by text that morning that there was going to be more than one baby. Both of us had thought there would be and so did my mum. We had also both thought that it was going to be an internal scan due to the short length of the pregnancy so far, so I wasn't going to be going in with her. But, the nurse came out after a few minutes to say that it was going to be external, and I could come and have a look.

And there it was! A little shape on the screen with a flickering fast heartbeat. I was overjoyed. There was just one baby and the nurse said that everything looked perfect. I must have looked like a really proud father and the nurse printed off a couple of pictures for me. I have to say that when I look at them now, I can't really make out much apart from something that looks like a transparent fish with an eye in it. The nurse confirmed for us that the baby would be due at the beginning of December 2010. An early Christmas present!

Kerry and I didn't hang around for long; she was off college for the week and I wanted to get back to Edinburgh. We did have a good hug and I felt extremely happy. I had worried about making it to this stage, especially considering the problems that Kerry had had in the past, but we had made it!

I made a few calls on the way home; mainly to let people know there was one baby in there and also that all seemed to be very healthy.

Oddly, the son of my parents' neighbours was going through the IVF process with his wife. She couldn't conceive naturally, so they had the same treatment as us, at exactly the same time. She was going for her scan that same day as well and I later found out that they too were expecting one baby, although they had thought it might be two.

Once back home, I showed the scan pictures to Marc and there was nothing but a mild response; I think a half-hearted smile was all I got in fact. This was just so bloody frustrating – I wanted to be able to get wildly excited about it, go out and look at baby clothes and prams and toys and nappies. All I could do was sit quietly at home and just act like there was nothing extraordinary going on. It was just all so wrong and upsetting.

*   *   *

For the next couple of weeks, Kerry was pretty quiet. I did text her a couple of times, but didn't receive much, if any, response. She sent me a text on Saturday 17 April to let me know that she had the twelve-week scan booked in for 20 May. I was down in Blackpool for the weekend and when the text came through it perked me up. I checked with her if this was the scan where you could tell the baby's sex and she said it was too early – that would be the sixteen-week scan. There was my lack of patience showing through again.

I texted her again after my weekend in Blackpool and was quite taken aback at her response. I'd just sent the usual 'how you doing' text, to which she replied that she had been in bed since the weekend and felt like crap, and wasn't really in the mood for texting. But she would let me know when she was. I didn't quite know what to make of that, but I just let it go.

Then, on Thursday 22 April, I heard from her again. As she had been ill, she was told to go for another scan, but all was fine and she was feeling a lot better. She also sent through two pictures of the new scans to my phone. This really perked me up and made my day, and week! The scan pictures showed a much bigger blob than the last time and these ones showed little stumps, which I managed to work out were the baby's arms and legs.

During the ninth week, on 28 April 2010, Kerry phoned me in a bit of a panic. She had been doing a report on surrogacy for her studies at college and had found that her husband needed to be named on the birth certificate when the baby was born. This came as a bolt out of the blue for me; I always thought she would be named as the mother and me as the father, and then that would be that! But no; these things have to be complicated. From what she had said, it seemed that, as she is married, her husband had to be the named father initially as far as she knew. Then we would have to get a parental order filled out and filed with a court after the baby is six weeks old. Once that all goes through, a new birth certificate would be issued with the details of the intended parents.

After a little research, the literature I found just confirmed what Kerry had said according to English law. I couldn't quite believe that Emma hadn't told anyone about this in the first place. Not that it was such a major issue for me, but it would have been nice for me to be able to go and sign the register of births like other dads get to do, so finding this out now brought about a little bit of disappointment. It also meant that we would have more hoops to jump through before everything was finalised.

It was that night, Wednesday 28 April, a day after our fifth anniversary, that I decided enough was enough for me and Marc, and I left the house, and Marc. His attitude towards me that night had been appalling and I finally just flipped, told him that I didn't actually like him any more, and I said I was going to stay in a hotel. I was quite surprised at myself when I did this. His behaviour towards me had worsened in the past few weeks, but it was odd that a brief conversation at home was the straw that broke the camel's back.

The thought of leaving him petrified me somewhat, but in the middle of this whole process, I had decided that I couldn't realistically bring up a child in Edinburgh, with no family or support network locally, and no support from Marc whatsoever. Also, bringing a child into a relationship where I felt there was only going to be one willing parent was just not going to work. I could imagine various scenarios based around the fact that Marc wasn't the child's real dad, so he didn't have to take real responsibility. This was me thinking negatively at its worst!

Leaving Marc also raised the issue of the parental order, where seemingly it isn't as straightforward to get one when the intended parent is single. But that was something I would need to talk to a lawyer about.

As far as I was concerned at the time, it was time for us both to move on with our lives and for me to start planning ahead. Time for a fresh start! I was feeling so emotional about the whole situation and at the time I just couldn't think of anything else to do. My feelings of loneliness even when I was with Marc were compounded by bitterness and a lack of desire for me to start talking to him about things again. I just couldn't cope with it all any more.

After my night in the hotel, and a difficult day at work, I went back to the house. Marc was supposed to be going to a work's quiz for the night, but when I arrived home at 6.00 p.m., he was upstairs looking out of the bedroom window. I had no idea what to expect, but I went in feeling quite headstrong. We had a chat as soon as I got in and I was very honest about the fact that this time it felt as if there was no going back. I explained that the way he had been treating me had made me not like him very much, and I couldn't allow that to keep happening. He told me that he didn't know why he did but that didn't really help me at all.

We then moved on to talking about the baby. It turned out that he had agreed to this in the first place because he didn't want to lose me, and that he only ever saw the whole process leading to a child that would be mine, not his. I was really disappointed when he said this and explained that this was supposed to be about the two of us, which was always what I had wanted from the start – our own family. If I had known about his feelings from the beginning, I would never ever have gone ahead with it. I certainly wouldn't have left him if he had said no to the whole thing in the first place; I would have dealt with it in my own way and we would have got over it.

But, now that he had said what he said, it made things much clearer in my head. There could be absolutely no going back now even if I wanted to; I just couldn't contemplate bringing a child into a relationship where one half of the couple didn't feel any responsibility towards him or her.

So, that was that. We did talk around some other issues and he kept making the point that in five years we had nothing to show for our relationship. But I disagreed with this, as we had done a lot together; I supported him through his degree, we built up our property portfolio and had some fun along the way. It wasn't all bad.

When we had finished talking, I gave him the choice of which bed he wanted for the night, and he took the double. That was fine with me at the time. It was quiet from 9.00 p.m. onwards; he spent some time sitting on the bed and then watched a bit of telly. I was in my bed by 11.00 p.m., shattered, starving and wondering what on earth life was going to bring along next. The situation between us wasn't resolved at the time, we hadn't agreed who would move out and when, and that left some uncertainty in my head, and some discomfort in terms of how we actually separate ourselves from each other. But I expected that would all come in good time.

Panic Again

Just when I thought everything was going fantastically well with the baby itself, on Friday 30 April, late afternoon, I received the following text from Kerry:

'Hi, David. I have sent Emma a text. I'm not happy with the situation I have been put in and if I'd known I would not have gone ahead with everything. I have requested a copy of the contract signed by you as I never received one from the beginning.'

I immediately started to panic and was thinking the worst, so I quickly sent Kerry a message to see if we could talk. She agreed, so I called her and there was an element of fear in her voice. After a while chatting, I think I got to the bottom of the issue. She had asked Emma for a copy of the contract a couple of weeks before and hadn't received it. She also hadn't had the life insurance that was promised. I had paid Emma for this some months ago and she obviously still hadn't sorted it out. This was pretty typical of Emma; I had always known she wasn't the best at organising things at the right time, and this really just confirmed it for me.

The main issue, though, seemed to be all the practical and legal arrangements: things such as the birth certificate and also what would happen at the hospital when the baby was born. She clearly didn't want any involvement with the child at all once it appeared and was afraid that she would have to spend time with it, which she didn't want to do.

I didn't know what to say to give her any reassurances, but I suddenly thought that getting a lawyer involved might help, probably for both of us. Once back at my desk at work, I found a lawyer in Edinburgh and made an appointment for 5.30 p.m. on Thursday 6 May. I was relieved that I had managed to sort this out and I sent Kerry a text to let her know. I also asked if she wanted to be put in touch with a surrogate who had done this before, but she didn't respond to that.

Later that night, I sent another text asking if she wanted to meet with the lawyer herself, but she said no; it would be fine. She also confirmed that the real issue she wanted to find out about was the one relating to the birth certificate. I decided I would contact her again, probably on Thursday before I went to the lawyer, to check if there was anything else she wanted me to ask about.

I felt quite a bit better by the end of the night!

The following Monday, I was at work and decided to call Emma just to see if she had managed to speak to Kerry. She told me that she had and that the midwife had confused Kerry, as she hadn't dealt with a surrogacy case before. Emma explained to me that she or a lawyer can write to the hospital to confirm that this is a surrogacy case and that the letter will explain the situation and ensure that the baby isn't handed over to Kerry, and that she doesn't have to have anything to do with the child. She had explained this to Kerry and also said to me that Kerry was probably very hormonal. (This seemed like a real understatement at the time.) Seemingly, all was now fine with Kerry and she was happy with Emma's explanation.

This gave me a lot of reassurance, as I was still feeling pretty bad about it up to that point. Panic over! Although I did still plan to go and see the lawyer anyway, just for some clarity about the issues for myself, as well as Kerry.

Single Dad

So, panic over and life was about to move on. Over the next few days, Marc was starting to look for somewhere else to live and making the odd remark about having to live by himself, and strange comments about me having someone to get up for in the morning. I found it odd that he was saying things like that, as he would always have Rebecca, and I said that to him, although he then replied that it wasn't the same. I felt like replying that it was his choice to leave Aberdeen when he did all those years ago, but I left it. I didn't want to hurt him or make him feel bad. I knew that he had enough on his plate, partly due to my decision.

It was at this point that the reality of the changes I would have to make over next few months started to hit home. At the time, we had two Rottweilers – Keira and Diesel. Firstly, I had decided that Diesel, our male dog, was going to have to be rehomed in advance of the baby coming. He was a lovely dog, only about 18 months old at the time, and full of fun, energy and affection. But, he was just too excitable and had already demonstrated his need for constant attention from Marc and me, to the point that we couldn't give Keira any attention without Diesel jumping on us (albeit in a friendly way). But, I just wouldn't trust him around a baby, and with the prospect of being a single dad coming up, I couldn't ever imagine having the ability to walk two dogs and carry a baby at the same time. So, I sat down in the office and advertised him on two websites. I wasn't looking for any money for him, just a good loving home where he would get all the attention he craves. I was fighting back the tears when I was doing this, but I knew it had to happen. Plus, with the expectation of Marc leaving the house soon, it would make my life a lot easier in the interim period. It did bring it all home to me, though, the prospect of moving to and living in Blackpool – one dog, one baby and my family close at hand. Scary thoughts – the worst of which was not having Marc in my life.

Legal Stuff

On the morning of 6 May, I was looking forward to my meeting with the lawyer. I'd started to type out some questions that I knew needed to be covered and I kept these in my bag ready for later. Then I realised that I'd missed a phone call from him. I called him to find out what was up and he told me that he would have to cancel and couldn't meet me until the following week, so I thought I'd best ask him the main question there and then, so at least I could let Kerry know what the answer was.

The lawyer was great. He really knew his stuff and confirmed that there was no reason for Kerry's husband, Tony, to go on the birth certificate. His approach in all surrogacy cases was to ensure that at least one of the intended parents had legal responsibility for the child from day one, and that he should always get at least the natural father's name on the birth certificate. He said that he had a template agreement which all parties needed to sign, so that there was no ambiguity about any of the process, and he would talk me through this when we met.

So, we arranged that I would go to meet him on Wednesday 12 May at 5.30 p.m. again. I felt so much better after talking to him.

I wondered how best to contact Kerry to let her know what the lawyer had said. I had sent her a text the night before asking how she was doing and she hadn't responded, so I assumed she was either out of credit or still in a bad mood about it all. I decided just to phone her instead and surprisingly, she did answer, so I relayed the whole conversation with the lawyer to her as quickly as I could speak. I could feel my heart pounding as I was talking to her; I was that worried about not getting the reaction I had wanted, or even worse, getting a nasty reaction.

Thankfully, though, she was as reassured as I was by what the lawyer had said, and I could hear in her voice a sense of relief; we even had a bit of a laugh. I told her how much I had been panicking about the idea that this could have been a show stopper, but she told me she would never have aborted the pregnancy, which I confessed had been at the back of my mind for a few days now.

Finally, we agreed that I would take the draft agreement along to the hospital when I went for the scan with her on the 20 May, as she had no computer access at all just then. And that was that – panic over, again!

Making Myself Comfortable

The closer we got to twelve weeks (the apparently 'safe time'), the more I started to realise how little I knew about bringing up a baby. Even the essentials, such as feeding and nappy changing were pretty alien to me. So, I decided I should buy some books. I didn't have any other option as I knew of nobody locally who could give me practical hands-on experience. There was Marc, but at that stage I didn't feel like I could ask him anything at all.

So, on 8 May, after the traumatic experience of re-homing Diesel, I went into town and bought a copy of *You're the Daddy* by Stephen Giles. I was quite looking forward to reading it, as it would be my first real insight into fatherhood, even thought it was a light-hearted book. I'd ordered another book through Amazon the previous day, which would cover all the practicalities, but I thought I would leave reading that one until nearer the time.

I managed to read some of the book over the weekend and it provided useful information about the father's experience of having a baby. It didn't go into too much detail, but I found it useful reading nonetheless.

That weekend, however, was ruined somewhat by the return of Diesel, which frustrated me as I thought I had taken one step closer to my new life by re-homing him, and then had to take a step back again once he was back home. Some silly people just decided he wasn't for them and made up some excuse about their daughter being frightened of him.

On the Monday 10 May, Marc had gone to bed and I was in the mood to communicate, so I sent messages to a few of my old pals to let them know about the baby. I thought it was safe enough now, as we were in our twelfth week. I got a few messages back, mostly of shock and disbelief, but all supportive and excited. Joan, my old neighbour in London, actually phoned the next day, wondering if I had gone straight. I had to laugh and explained to her what had happened. She promised a few trips to Blackpool in the future. I was going to look forward to that. I also spoke to my old friend Wally that night, after he called to find out what was going on, so I gave him an update. He also asked if I had turned straight. This is a subject that was often on my mind – not about whether I could turn straight (which I definitely couldn't), but that I was going to end up with a very straight lifestyle or, at least, it wouldn't be a gay one. When I finished reading my first baby book that Tuesday, I also quickly came to the conclusion that I wasn't going to have much time to myself, never mind enough time to go out socialising and partying! It was all going to be such a culture shock. By the sounds of it, life would be filled with nappy changing, health visitors, feeding, trying to get some sleep and bonding with the baby.

I knew that I was going to have to get some help from the family, as spending the majority of my time in the house with my son or daughter could become quite lonely without adult interaction. It would also be good to have someone else to change a nappy every now and again.

More Panic!

I'd sent a text message to Kerry at lunchtime on Wednesday 12 May to see if she was okay and also to ask if she wanted to chat before I went along to see the lawyer for my meeting. I didn't hear back from her quickly though, which wasn't out of the ordinary, as she often took her time, if she replied at all.

At 3.30 p.m., I noticed I had just missed a call from her and when I finally got hold of her, she told me something that scared me to death. The night before, she had had a small bleed and she had been worried that she was about to miscarry. She hadn't slept all night and just lay on the bed feeling guilty. That morning, she had been to her doctor who referred her for an immediate scan at the hospital, and she had just come out when she tried to call me. Thankfully, everything was okay and she even saw the baby sucking his or her thumb on the monitor.

I must have gone through a whole enormous range of emotions during that conversation: from panic, to worry, to fear, back to panic and then to relief. She told me that the consultant at the hospital explained what the bleed was about. It looked like the other embryos, the ones that were implanted with the successful one, were probably just coming away now, but the baby was perfectly healthy and everything looked absolutely fine. She had got four more scan pictures to show me, which she'd give me the following week.

We talked for a while about what would have happened if things had gone pear-shaped, and whether we would do it again. I told her I would, as we had gone through so much together and learnt a lot about the process that I'd be comfortable, and in fact a repeat run would probably be much more straightforward now that we knew everything that was involved. I had everything crossed that we wouldn't need to even think about that, unless I wanted the baby to have a brother or sister later on down the line. That is a long way off!

So, it was a short-lived panic, but it was panic all the same and it left me thinking a lot more about the fact that this still could all go wrong, and maybe I was getting too excited too early, but there was nothing much I could do about that. Whatever was going to happen would happen.

This was the night I was due to take Diesel to Fife Rottweiler Rescue. I can't imagine what I would have done if Kerry had told me that she had miscarried.

Meeting the Lawyer

My meeting with the lawyer was quite useful. Although I have to say that he didn't tell me much that I didn't already know. He went through the whole legal side of the surrogacy process and confirmed for me some of the technical details.

On the subject of the birth certificate, he confirmed that I should go with Kerry to register the birth and that he had never encountered a problem with this before, as it is quite common (i.e. separated wives who have children with their new partners but who haven't any formal separation or divorce in place).

We went on to talk about the fact that I wanted to take the baby to Blackpool as soon as it was born, and he clarified that if we were going to apply for a parental order in Scotland, then I would have to stay in Scotland with the baby until the order was granted. This presented a difficulty for me, as there was no way that I wanted to start life with the baby outside of Blackpool by myself. I would have to stay in Glasgow until we were able to register the birth, which was bad enough, but at least that would just be for a couple of days. I asked the lawyer to look into this further for me.

He agreed to pull together a draft legal agreement which covered all the aspects of the surrogacy that we would encounter from then on, i.e. how the handover of the baby is managed, how quickly we register the birth and other things. He told me that this would be with me over the next couple of days, so I could have a read and take it to Kerry the following week.

I called Kerry later that day and went through what the lawyer had said; she was fine with it all and we had a good laugh and a joke. She was telling me that she was already massive and that she was used to giving birth to big babies. I explained that I was over 9lb when I was born, which caused her to threaten me with a kick up the arse. We were laughing about it, but she did say that she was generally always early anyway, so it might not be a problem.

Onwards and Upwards

By Thursday 13 May, we were just two days short of being twelve weeks pregnant. Kerry sent a few messages that morning saying how she thought it was a boy. She had done her checks through the Chinese lunar calendar (not that I buy into any of that), and bearing in mind my birth year and the egg donor's, it should be a boy. She also had a feeling it was a boy, although she did say that this was just a feeling, rather than based on any sort of objective measure.

That day, she sent me a picture of the latest scan to my phone, and it did actually look like a baby this time, sucking its thumb, and he or she was a lot bigger than on the last scan. It still wasn't too clear, but it looked a lot better than the last one.

All was well with the world as far as the baby was concerned. The next step I was looking forward to was the scan in Glasgow, booked for Thursday 20 May at 9.45 a.m.

I spent that weekend in Blackpool and the Saturday was a real milestone – we had made it to twelve full weeks of pregnancy! I think I was so overjoyed about events of the previous week that my excitement didn't really register, although I did talk to Mum about baby things and my sister had been rooting through her attic and finding a load of old baby things, such as an old car seat and clothes. Seemingly, the cot was at my parents' house somewhere as well.

That Sunday, back in Edinburgh, I texted Kerry just to check if it was okay for me to start buying baby things now that we were past twelve weeks, and I received a light-hearted response, so all was well. I also started reading my newest book, *A Rough Guide to Babies*. It is geared towards new mums, but this baby isn't going to have a mum in its life, so I was going to have to learn all of this stuff (except the chapters about breast-feeding, postnatal depression and how to deal with neglected husbands – or maybe I would need to know a bit about that). The book is very good and deals with a lot of the practical stuff: dos and don'ts, and lots of different options for doing all sorts of things. It opened my eyes a bit to say the least, and kept me interested until just before midnight when I finally gave up. One thing that stuck in my mind from the book was that if you have a boy and are changing his nappy, keep a towel over his willy until you get the new nappy on, as he would be liable to shoot a fountain of pee into the air. I was looking forward to watching that happen (if it turned out to be a boy).

The Twelve-Week Scan

The next scan, booked for 20 May, was a real milestone for me. I was extremely excited as this was going to be the first time I would see the baby actually looking like a baby.

The appointment, at the Southern General in Glasgow, was booked for the early hours of the morning, so I decided to go west the night before to miss the horrendous traffic between Edinburgh and Glasgow. I stayed the night at the Travel Lodge in Braehead, and it felt like I was in the middle of nowhere; the hotel was at the edge of the retail park at Braehead and was a nice enough hotel, but for the fact that it had no character, soul or atmosphere. Plus, there was no outside seating, so I ended up taking a bottle of wine outside onto the car park and sitting down on the ground next to a skip, where I drank and smoked and made phone calls all night. All too soon, it was after 1.00 a.m., so I went to bed and was full of excitement about the next morning.

The alarm went off at what felt like the middle of the night and I was raring to go to the hospital to see Kerry and my baby. Kerry turned up at the same time as me and we walked into the place together. We had a catch up in the waiting room and she was telling me about the holiday she had booked at the end of September, and the fact that she hated being abroad when she was pregnant. She also doesn't like sand or water, which made me wonder why on earth she was going. Each to their own, I suppose.

It wasn't long before we were called into the room where the scan was due to happen. And there it was – my baby – alive and very much kicking. It was such an awesome sight to see, this little baby, shaped like a little baby and wriggling about, moving its legs and arms about and opening and closing its mouth. All I could do was stare at the screen, watching in absolute amazement. It was twelve and a half weeks old and according to the nurse who did the scan, it all looked absolutely perfect. Its fingers and toes were all in place, it had such long legs that every now and again it would kick into the air, and it kept on moving its arms around and looked like it was sucking its thumb.

The nurse was trying to measure various parts of its body, but it wouldn't get into the right position for her to measure its head, so she was pushing the scanner into Kerry's belly to get it to move, and it took ages. She had to ask Kerry to go and empty her bladder to see if that would help and after a few more minutes of struggling, she finally got what she wanted. It was such an amazing experience; I could have sat there for hours watching.

When Kerry was out of the room, I asked the nurse about the sex of the baby. She told me that if it's a boy and he lies in a certain position with his legs open, you can see the start of his willy being formed. Today, the baby didn't lie in such a position, so I would need to wait until the next scan. My patience seemed to be under control at that point, as I didn't seem to mind. I managed to take some great scan pictures away with me and was looking forward to being able to show them to the people that mattered.

From that point on, the rest of the morning was mainly spent sitting around and waiting. Kerry had to go for various appointments with the midwife and a doctor to talk through her medical history, and also to tell them about the fact this was a surrogacy. I think they were a bit taken aback; they had obviously never dealt with surrogacy before, so didn't know what to do. I was a bit shocked when the midwife told me she would need to inform Social Services, but I supposed at that point that they were only covering their back. It did worry me slightly, but I tried to put it out of my mind. Shortly after that, the same midwife said I should contact them for some parenting classes, which I thought was nice and planned to follow her advice later in the process.

Still in the hospital at 1.00 p.m., I was starting to feel shattered, over-heated and tetchy, so I nipped out for a fag. Just as I was lighting up, Kerry texted to say I needed to go in and give some blood. This was for a test to check antibodies, to ensure that Kerry's body wouldn't reject the child because of its blood – or something. So, I went into the consulting room with Kerry, took off half of my sweater (which I really shouldn't have worn in view of the heat) and the doctor proceeded to take three vials of blood. It was sore afterwards, but it had to be done I suppose. Then, after a couple more minutes, that was us done. Kerry and I had a quick chat outside and then went on our way. I was exhausted, so God knows how she must have felt.

The next time we talked, I realised that it was going to be another two months before I found out the baby's sex. I thought the next scan would be at sixteen weeks, but it wasn't – it was at twenty weeks! Two more months! Bloody hell! I wanted to be able to decide on names. I knew it was probably going to be either Evan Vincent for a boy or Erin Anna for a girl, with another middle name so her initials aren't EAR. I did think of trying to come up with a Scottish name for both of them, but after thinking of Heather (not sure if it's Scottish) and Hamish, I gave up for a while. Mind you, there's always Fraser and Ailie.

The next thing for us to do was agree to the content of the legal agreement, which still hadn't come through. The hospital had said that they needed to see it, but that it could wait until the next scan. At least that took the pressure off and I was sure we could get it sorted in the next couple of weeks, as long as the lawyer pulled his finger out.

I didn't get home until just before 6.00 p.m., and obviously showed Marc the scan pictures. Yet again, the response I received was 'Jolly good.' I didn't pursue the matter; I just asked him to scan them into his computer so that I could email them to the family. I was looking forward to their reaction and as expected, it was a positive one full of excitement and fun, which helped me maintain my positive mood as well.

After this, I went through the 'new-born package' that the hospital had sent me home with. All I found in there of any use was one nappy, the tiniest pots of Sudocrem in the world and a sachet of Ovaltine. There were a couple of semi-useful vouchers, which I intended to make use of at some point, but the rest of it was thrown into the recycling boxes. It was all adverts and a lot of it was about breast-feeding, a source of much guilt for me, so I didn't spend much time reading it.

The evening was a quick one for me and apart from tea and a dog walk, I didn't do much else but have some email chatter with my sister and brother, and watch some crap on TV. It had been a shattering day and after reading some of my book in bed, I had my light out at 11.00 p.m. and must have been dead to the world a few minutes later.

On the Friday of that week, the draft legal agreement finally arrived from the lawyer and I was pretty pleased with it. The agreement we had originally received from Emma was totally different and it didn't cover any of the legal stuff that should have been in there. I spent a couple of hours tinkering with the new one, as it should have been signed before any of the surrogacy process had taken place. So, I changed it to reflect the fact that we were now halfway through the process and emailed it back to the lawyer over the weekend for him to approve. Thankfully, he replied quickly on Monday morning, saying that what I had done was fine. So, that was another obstacle overcome. I posted it to Kerry that night, hoping that it would be another step to making her 100% comfortable about the whole legal process.

More Trouble

I knew that this whole process was never going to be easy, but so many times I was sent into panic mode …

On Tuesday 25 May, Kerry texted me to say that she had spent some time in hospital at the weekend, as she had started bleeding again. She said they had done another scan and all was fine, and that she had another picture for me. She also told me that she was still losing some blood, but the hospital had assured her that there was nothing to worry about. This scare made me think that maybe I shouldn't have assumed that all was going to go according to plan. I had told so many people about the baby and couldn't face telling them if it all went wrong. I would hate it and myself if that happened. In fact, I just didn't know what I would do. All sorts of thoughts were going through my head yet again and I decided not to let anyone know what she had told me. I didn't want anyone else worrying as much as I was doing.

However, one positive did come from our conversation that day; she told me that we now had the date for the twenty-week scan – it was to be on 12 July at 2.00 p.m., so that was something to look forward to. At least now it was booked I felt that we had to get to that stage.

In the meantime, we were verging on completing the legal agreement. On Wednesday 26 May, the lawyer confirmed that he had sent a letter to Kerry, and also the draft agreement as amended by me. On the Thursday, Kerry and I spoke about it. She was very happy with it, so that was one hurdle nearly over. I agreed to get in touch with the lawyer to find out how we went about signing it, and emailed him that day.

Kerry was in a perky mood, which was good as it put me

in a good mood as well. Also, the bleeding seemed to have stopped – another positive.

The lawyer finally emailed through a final version of the agreement on the following Wednesday. I immediately sent it off to Kerry so she could sign it and send it back to me. Hopefully that was the end of the legalities for the time being.

Shopping!

I had thought that by 5 June I would have known whether it was a boy or girl, but I had to wait until 12 July for that. However, I'd put a note in my diary to go shopping for baby things on the fifth, and I did still want to be able to go out and buy things, so I did! I headed over to the shopping centre in Livingstone and I had a look around a few shops.

For some reason, it felt a little weird. Buying baby things just didn't feel natural at all, and I just didn't enjoy the experience. After looking at baby-grows in a few shops, I got the impression that I wasn't going to be able to buy anything that was plain – everything seemed like it was either for a boy or girl. But finally, I managed to find some packs of white baby-grows for newborns in Marks and Spencers, and paid £12 for two packs. That was all I bought and was glad it was over. I had thought at that stage that it was probably best to wait until 12 July to buy anything else.

I did also go to Halfords, where I wanted to have a look at car seats for the baby, but I felt totally out of my depth. I had a good look and eventually picked up a booklet which would hopefully help me. There are so many rules and things to consider about baby seats; it wasn't long before I gave up.

On the Monday night, 7 June, I was having a chat with my sister and she was asking if I minded if she bought some things for the baby. That made me smile and put me in a good mood for the rest of the night.

More Scans

On Wednesday 9 June, I was working at home and had planned to call Kerry during the day to see how she was doing. Oddly, she called me early in the morning to let me know that she had received a letter at her house addressed to me, from the clinic in Cyprus, asking what I wanted to do about the other embryos in storage. There was a cost of about €990 a year to keep them.

There was no way I could decide at that stage whether I would want any more children after this one was born. I did try and give it some thought but it was just way too early. I decided if I gave myself another year that would mean baby number one would be a few months old and by that stage, I would know how I felt about the whole thing.

Kerry and I had a good chat on the phone, which was nice. She was telling me about the way her hormones made her feel and that she had been quite tearful the week before. She said she sometimes felt like she was not in control of her own body, and that I was calling the shots. I did find it quite odd, but I told her she needed to let me know if there was anything she needed me to do differently; if I wasn't in contact with her enough, or too much, then I'd be happy to change. I told her I'd just go along with whatever she wanted. She also told me that she'd been having a bit more of a bleed and so arranged to go for a scan the next day. She said she would let me know afterwards if all was okay.

On the Thursday morning, she texted to say everything was fine, so I gave her a quick ring. She said that the hospital seemed a bit pissed off that she had gone for a scan again, but she wasn't too sure why. The baby looked fine and was jumping around like mad, though they hadn't told her the sex, as it must have been too early.

Then, on the Friday, the signed legal agreement arrived back from Kerry. So, all there was to do now was for me and Marc to sign it and send it back to the lawyer. That felt like another milestone – all the legalities done and we are almost halfway through the pregnancy. Yippee!

I had to ask Marc on the Thursday night if he would be happy to sign it, given the current situation. He had decided that he was moving out on the following Sunday and I was due to be away all weekend, so he quickly read it and then signed it. That night in the house was not a good one; there was quite a lot of upset about the fact that he was moving out and it felt like we really were coming to an end – a fact that saddened me deeply. I don't think he ever knew how much I loved him and if he did, it never showed. I was feeling pretty gutted inside.

Sunday, when Marc moved out, was an awful day. I'd been thinking about him all weekend and where we went wrong. I'd known things hadn't been right for a while and had tried my best to fix things, but it just never worked, regardless of the efforts I made. This day was probably the start of a big change in me.

I had the agreement witnessed over the weekend by my mum and posted it off, recorded delivery, to the lawyers on the Monday, and that was it – done and dusted! I did think I should have just dropped it through the letterbox at the lawyers myself, as they were only on Queen Street, which was almost on my way home from work, but at least sending it by recorded delivery would give me proof of posting.

The whole of the next week, I didn't hear from Kerry at all. I'd sent her a friendly text message on the Friday, but had no response.

On Saturday 19 June, I headed down to Blackpool again with the dog for the weekend to see the family and it was good. My mum surprised me by showing me a load of baby stuff she had bought – wipes, bibs and other useful items – and my sister also took me to her place where she had dug out a whole load of things from when my nephews were babies. There was a mass of stuff – a car seat, toys, a whole shop full of clothes, baby-grows and everything you could think of. She also had a rocking cradle, which she said I could have, and I took it with me in the car. I wanted to be able to re-assemble it, so that was something I would look forward to when I got back to Edinburgh. I know it was a bit daft taking it all that way back when I would just have to move it back to Blackpool again, but it was just something I wanted to do.

Back in Edinburgh on Sunday, I ploughed through a load of housework and saved building the cradle until last. It was easy to build and I was quite proud of myself once I'd done it. I just had to go out and find a mattress for it now, which I'd planned to do that afternoon. I should really have taken measurements, but I never got round to it, so I just had a quick look round Mamas and Papas at the Craigleith shopping centre, before going for the open viewing at the flat I was selling in Liddesdale Place.

The rest of the afternoon was quite a stressful one; Marc was back at the house again, packing more things up and taking some stuff with him, and by this stage, we weren't really getting on at all. Once he had done what he had to do, he handed me his keys and left. It was all very upsetting, but it still didn't feel as if it was really over at that stage. I had a room full of all his things, plus there was loads of his stuff in the garage and I didn't have any closure to the whole situation at all. It felt really unnatural and wrong.

A Beating Heart

Thankfully, on Monday 22 June, I heard from Kerry at last. A text came through at lunchtime saying, 'Just had a prenatal appointment. Heard your baby's heartbeat.' Well, that certainly put a smile on my face. So, I thought I would give her a call and have a chat with her. She seemed to be in a good mood that day and was telling me she was getting fat again, which we had a laugh about. She was also trying to tell me about the results of the blood tests, but all I could make out was that everything was fine. She was telling me that the heartbeat was 143 beats per minute, which was good for the stage we were at. I did check to see if she wanted to meet up before the scan on 12 July, but she said she had loads on between now and then, so we should leave it. I didn't take this negatively, though, as at least I was reassured that all was fine.

I felt so much better after speaking to her, and it put me in a positive frame of mind. So, I had to call my mum and let her know the news, not that it was that exciting, and it still didn't give me any clues as to the sex of the baby. I was still thinking at this point that it was a boy, though, and oddly, so did most other people.

The official copies of the legal agreements arrived on Tuesday 22 June. So, that was all done and dusted. Also, that same day, I emailed the clinic in Cyprus to confirm that I wanted the embryos to remain in storage, and that I would send money through to them at the end of the month. It worked out at about €50, as the rest of the charge was for them storing my sperm, which seemed a bit pointless and very expensive for such a little amount.

On a day off on 25 June, Kerry was texting and it was all fun. She was asking how much I was looking forward to the

78

scan and trying to get me to set up a Facebook account. I eventually managed the Facebook thing on a day working from home on Tuesday 29 June, although I'm not really sure why I did it. I linked to family, Kerry, my ex, Darren, and some of his family, as well as a couple of old school pals.

That next week started out so slowly. With the enormity of what was going to happen the following Monday, finding out the sex of the baby, by myself, I started to get pretty worried. I had spoken to my sister on the phone and I got all upset, and called her back the next night to apologise. This was also the week I was aiming to give up smoking. I foolishly advertised the fact on Facebook, so I couldn't really stop giving up once I had started even if I wanted to. When I thought about the fact that I was going to have a baby to live for, I realised that smoking really shouldn't have been happening at all. Can you imagine if I was diagnosed with some sort of smoking-related disease, or even cancer, before he or she was born? What a nightmare that would have been.

It was also this week that I told my boss at work about the baby. I think it was just an impulsive moment really, but my thinking was something along the lines of 'it's one less thing for me to worry about'. So, we'd had one of our regular one-to-one meetings arranged, went through our normal business and then I told her. Her initial reaction when I told her that I was going to be a dad was that she thought my dog was going to have puppies! After we resolved that one, she was actually really supportive and I don't suppose I expected anything else from her. I told her the whole story – well, a much briefer version of it at least – and we had a bit of a chat about my options in terms of work. She suggested that, even though it was not strictly the same, I might qualify for adoption pay and leave. I wasn't sure that I'd be that lucky, as it is quite a generous package, but she agreed to give the matter some thought and said that she would probably get back to me during the following week. I felt quite positive, having told her about it all, though I did say I didn't want anyone else to know at that stage. We discussed her telling her boss, and for some reason, I decided against it at that stage.

The Twenty-Week Scan

The weekend before the scan, I'd spent some time with Marc and he'd told me that he wanted to come along to the scan. I never really worked out the reasons, but I expect I was probably glad of the support. Plus, it still looked as though we were together to the people that mattered. Marc, up to now, hadn't taken much of a role in the whole process. By this stage, he hadn't shown any interest in being involved in any of it, and certainly no excitement about the fact that a baby was on the way. There was no expectation from either of us by now that he would be involved in bringing up the child, and although he had agreed to sign the legal paperwork, we both knew that this was really just a formality, and not an indication of any future commitment at all. All the same, he arrived at the house just after 12.00 p.m. on 12 July and we set off to Glasgow, with me full of excitement about finding out what sex the baby would be.

We probably set off too early, as we made it there by 1.15 p.m., so we went for a wander around the Sainsbury's at Braehead and I had a peek at some baby clothes, wishing I knew which sex to buy for.

We finally met Kerry at the hospital just before 2.00 p.m. and she looked so different; she was actually wearing a maternity dress and her bump was a lot bigger than the last time I had seen her. Her hair was down and she looked well.

The three of us sat in the waiting room for a short while, chatting and making small talk. She was about to get another puppy and then start breeding, and she was complaining about a skin condition caused by the pregnancy, which was preventing her from having her eyebrows threaded. Strange how I remember all these irrelevant details! But anyhow, her eyebrows looked fine to me!

Before long, we were in the scan room and it all started. I was just so excited. This was to be quite a detailed scan and as the nurse explained, it would be the one where they check for any signs of abnormality. Again, she took measurements of the baby's bones and skull, and it was just lovely to see its fingers and toes, and its arms and legs moving about. I could even make out its face and the nurse was pointing out its facial features, nose, eyes, lips and so on. She kept saying that it was a stubborn baby, as it wouldn't get into the position she needed to take certain measurements. She eventually got there, though.

All the way through this, she was checking for the sex organs. But, typical of my luck, the umbilical cord was in the way and she couldn't make them out clearly. I did get a bit frustrated, but there was absolutely sod all I could do about it. At one point when she looked, she said that she thought it was a girl. She could get slight glimpses of a structure which resembled the female sex organs, so she finally said that she would say 60% that it was a girl. And that was that – no definite answer. I think I felt a bit more gutted by the fact that I couldn't tell my mum or sister what the sex was, but it wasn't the end of the world.

The scan took about forty minutes in all and I got some good scan pictures again, especially one where I could see the profile of the baby's face. We then had to go and see the midwife. Last time we were there, a doctor had taken some blood so that they could do tests in relation to antibodies; Kerry had an antibody in her blood which might have reacted to a similar one in the baby and they needed to check it out. The blood they took the last time was wrongly labelled, so they had to take some more.

After waiting for what seemed like an eternity in a horrible waiting area full of expectant mothers trying to control their young children, we eventually got to see the midwife, Doreen. All three of us went in there and she took my blood as planned. We then had to talk about 'the plan': what was going to happen in the hospital when the baby was born. She proceeded to tell us that the baby needed to stay with its mother until both were ready to leave and all three of us basically told her that under no circumstances would the baby be staying with Kerry for any length of time at all.

After a lengthy discussion, Doreen agreed that she would speak to her bosses about what we could do; she would also find out from other hospitals what had happened in the past. She did admit that the whole scenario was new to her and the hospital, so she really didn't have a clue.

I left there feeling a bit disheartened; as usual, what should have been a positive day ended with frustration and disappointment. I tried talking to Marc about how he was now feeling about it all and whether he felt any differently about the baby now that he had seen it and been involved in the day's events, but it was obvious from his lack of emotion that he felt no different at all. I was disappointed about that and it probably marred my mood for the rest of the day.

Later that week, I gave Emma a ring to talk about this whole issue of the hospital and she said that she had worked with a couple in the past where the surrogate gave birth in a hospital in Scotland. She agreed to find out which hospital it was so that I could inform the hospital in Glasgow, but she never did get back to me about it. Nothing new there though!

A Disappointed Employee

On Thursday 15 July, I went to have a chat with my director and we got onto talking about the baby. My boss *had* told her about it the day before. My director was in fact very supportive at the time I spoke to her. She said I had been brilliant with the work I had done so far, and that I had the perfect skill set for the team. She also confirmed that in her new structure, there was a role that really played to my skills. I told her that I was really enjoying my job and would hate to have to leave, and that I would appreciate it if the university would be able to do something supportive for me in terms of paid leave. In response, she said that she would be able to let me know by the end of July what they could do, and expected that we would have a couple of discussions over the next couple of weeks about what would work for both the university and me. So, I came out of there feeling pretty positive about the whole thing.

The next day, my boss asked me for a chat and we went into her office. She told me that she had spoken to our Head of HR and they had decided to let me have one month off work with pay, two weeks of which would be the statutory paternity leave period. Any other time off would need to be on an unpaid basis. I did ask if she was prepared to go any further and she said no.

I was absolutely gutted. This response bore no resemblance to what my director had said the day before. I just wondered if this was my director saying what she thought I wanted to hear, but actually meaning something else. It really marred the rest of my day and made me wonder why I should bother doing as much work as I had been doing. What sort of loyalty to your employee is this? Absolutely shocking!

* * *

On Saturday 17 July, Marc and I were away for the weekend. This was supposedly about us trying to be friends and just getting away from all the horrible things that had gone on over the past few weeks. It was also a chance for me to escape from sitting indoors alone, drinking far too much, and actually have some fun. It turned out to be a fantastic weekend; Marc came over on the Friday after work and we had a good night chatting. On Saturday, Marc, myself and the dog packed ourselves up and headed up north to a place called Edzell: a small village somewhere near Brechin, near to Glen Esk. We had a whale of a time, walking, eating, enjoying the place and generally having a great time. In fact, it was just like old times, except that there were no rows, no bickering, just fun, getting out and about and having a laugh. We even talked about the baby, about what life could be like and how things might have worked if we were still together, getting up, taking the baby to nursery, going to work, etc. It was all nice and well meant. At one point, we even talked about getting back together, living in Edzell and what it could be like there.

Sadly, all good things must come to an end and it was soon time for us to leave. Coming home on Sunday, I was quite disappointed to leave. However, Marc wanted to stay over for the night with me, which again was nice (although I'm sure he only wanted to use the bath, as he didn't have a decent one where he was).

On the Monday morning, I visited the GP first thing; my previous attempts at giving up smoking had failed yet again, so I went along to see if I could get hold of some Champix: a drug which was supposed to help with the addiction. It worked in such a way that you carried on smoking while taking it and you would automatically want to stop in the second week. She gave me a two-week prescription for it, so I was quite chuffed.

Then, into work I went and as soon as I had the chance, I went in to see my director. I was still quite upset about what had happened on Friday, despite having had such a great weekend and feeling quite upbeat. I explained exactly how I felt about what had happened. I told her that I felt positive after our chat on Thursday, but after talking to my boss, I felt totally let down. My director was very apologetic; she explained that she hadn't told my boss what her thoughts were about my longer-term future with the university, and also that my boss was probably just looking at it all from a business perspective. I felt that I managed to get it all off my chest and felt better for it. My director said she was still keen to be supportive and we would get back together later on in the day to talk it through again after she had spoken with our local head of HR.

We arranged to meet again after lunch, but as luck would have it, she was free again at about 11.30 p.m., so in I went and I'm glad I did. She said that she would be more than happy to give me three months' paid leave and offer some flexibility if I needed more after that point. I was absolutely ecstatic. I really hadn't been expecting so much and I was so overjoyed. She said she was going to get this all confirmed in writing for me, so that it was made official and that would be that. I immediately phoned Marc to tell him and he sounded nearly as happy about it as I did.

As happy as I was, it did mean that I was going to have to sit down and think about what I was going to do about everything else; it meant a move to Blackpool was off the cards for now, but that I should consider moving house anyway within Edinburgh so that I could save some money.

I then looked into the university nursery to see what they could offer: full-time childcare from 8.30 p.m. to 5.30 p.m. for £873 per month! Ugh! However, they use a childcare voucher scheme which could save me £1,195 per year in tax and National Insurance, which made it sound a bit better. Oh, so much to think about. All good though – very good indeed!

I called Mum at lunchtime to let her know and she also sounded pretty chuffed, which made me feel even better. Things were on the up and I was feeling pretty proud of myself that day.

Towards the end of the day, my director emailed me just to give me some more reassurance about the whole thing, and even said how much she wanted me to stay. Things really were on the up.

That night, I spoke to my sister about it all and although she sounded fairly pleased, I sensed a little bit of disappointment in her voice about me not moving back to Blackpool straight away; either that, or she was distracted as she was doing the ironing at the same time as talking to me.

Making More Plans

I was in such a good mood when I went into work on Tuesday 20 July that I just needed to share it with someone, so I told my colleague, Irene about the baby. She seemed really chuffed for me. Irene had her only child when she was about my age and was really good to talk to about it all. Then I contacted one of our HR systems people to ask what the rules were about applying to get onto the Childcare Voucher Scheme. So, I had to tell her I was going to be a dad and she was full of the joys as well.

It turned out that I could start buying childcare vouchers and saving money on NI and tax quite quickly. So, I started that ball rolling. The way I was thinking was that if I save enough vouchers now, the first couple of nursery bills wouldn't be as hard to stomach. Plus, it meant that I was making the most of the scheme as far in advance as possible.

It didn't take long to go through the process of applying at all – just a quick online form to fill in and it was done. Seemingly, the university payroll team would do the rest.

My next job was to start looking at the property rental market, to see if there was anything as comfortable as my current home, but with less expensive rent, a better heating system, fewer bedrooms and cheaper council tax. I did see a couple that seemed okay, so I sent them through to Marc for him to have a look. It was probably too early to be doing anything about moving, but at least I was starting to have a look.

I also started planning a holiday, thinking that I would probably go to Mykonos in September that year for a couple of weeks. I managed to find a few good deals and the thought of getting away really excited me – two weeks on a beach with sun and sand and, erm, relaxation!

Towards the end of the day at work I started to think that maybe moving house wasn't such a good idea. Thinking about the stress of it all, coupled with the additional cost of moving, it somehow didn't seem worth it. If I ended up staying in Edinburgh then I would probably look to buy somewhere of my own in 2011, once one of my big loans had finished and the credit cards were paid off. Marc was due to come round for tea that night, so I thought I'd probably talk it through with him and see where I get to. We did chat it through, but it didn't help at all and we just ended up bickering about it for a bit, as Marc couldn't see my point of view.

By the Thursday of that week, I had the written confirmation from the university that they would give me twelve weeks paid special leave to care for the baby, and that provided some well-needed reassurance. I accepted their offer formally and also confirmed that I would take my outstanding annual leave before starting my period of special leave.

That day, I also decided that I really would stay in the house on Clermiston Road. Having worked out the finances, and also taken into account the stress of it all, it really wasn't worth moving at all. Plus, it meant that I would have a little more stability in my life.

Marc Again!

By this time, odd things were happening between Marc and me, and I really didn't know what to make of them. We had had a number of conversations over the previous few weeks about life and the baby, and I just couldn't work out what it was he wanted from it all, not helped by the fact that he kept saying that he didn't know either.

We had a recent discussion where he told me some of the issues he had about the baby. There were some financial ones, which I'd said I would generally take most responsibility for initially. There were some general responsibility issues, which there was nothing I could do about. And, there were some issues which, to use his words, were 'about the gayness of the whole thing'! I didn't know where to start with that one. He seemed to be worried about the way other people think in relation to two gay men bringing up a baby. I saw this as a bit of a challenge myself, but nothing that would ever have put me off. I always knew that there would the potential for some elements of discrimination, and there would be issues from people who had no experience of situations like this, but what other people thought really didn't matter to me. This baby would have as normal an upbringing as it possibly could without a mother. The fact that his or her dad is gay was irrelevant.

Marc had been up in Aberdeen the weekend of 24 July and I had my parents at the house. They left at lunchtime on the Sunday and Marc arrived at the house in the evening, and we had a really nice night together. This was the first time Marc had actually said that he wanted us to get back together, which I was really pleased about. I asked him if he had managed to clarify his thoughts about the baby, which he hadn't, but he did say that if we loved each other enough, we would be able to deal with anything. That put a big smile on my face, as he'd never really said anything like that before. However, we had both had a good drink that night and I did wonder to some extent whether it was the drink talking. So, the next morning, I asked if he had meant what he said the night before and he told me he meant every word of it.

As he was leaving, I asked when we were going to talk about things and we agreed he would come back over on Tuesday night after work to explore what would happen from thereon in. At that stage, I had no idea what this conversation was going to bring. I didn't know if he was really being sincere or if he wanted us to be together, but to live apart (which could never work), or what sort of relationship he actually wanted us to have.

I thought about it a lot that day, especially about how I would feel if we agreed to get back together, and the fact that in reality I would be getting what I had always previously wanted – the man I was in love with and my own little family. It also meant I wouldn't be a single dad after all, which would mean less of a panic about the impending months. I suppose, at that stage, I could only wait and see what would happen the next day. On a very positive note, we had agreed that we would be going on holiday together in September and had both booked the appropriate time off work that day. Yippee!

That night was a bit of a lonely one – just the dog Keira and me in the house. I did text Kerry to see if she had heard back from the midwife about the plan for the day of the birth, but she said she hadn't. She wasn't chatty or friendly at all in this exchange.

Marc and I?

Tuesday 27 July was quite a weird one throughout my working day. I was wondering what was going to happen when Marc came over that night. Was he going to change his mind about the whole thing? Was he going to present what he wanted on his terms and see if I agreed to it? It wasn't such a busy day at work, so I had plenty of time to think things through – never a good thing for me and the way my mind works. I was looking forward to him coming though, which was the main thing.

When we eventually talked about getting back together, we started with the baby. Seemingly, Marc had turned a corner in terms of dealing with his issues; he now saw it as manageable and wasn't as concerned about any of the discrimination issues. Oddly, he told me that he had mentioned us possibly getting back together to his daughter, Rebecca, and she had been upset about the fact that he would then be bringing up the baby. I found it strange that he hadn't told me this before, but he said that this was not something that would put him off coming back.

We then got onto other issues about us, at which point Marc said that although he wanted to come back, he wasn't sure if he was ready to do it just yet. He started telling me that there were things he wanted to do before he moved back in, such as going down to London for a few days and having some time away by himself. My impression was that this was about him making the most of his freedom while he still had it and I found this very difficult to deal with. I couldn't see how, if you are planning to get back into a relationship with someone, you still carry on as if you are single.

I told Marc that he should do what he wanted to do, and if that was it then so be it. I would deal with it in my own way; I just didn't know what that way was at that stage. Would I have wanted him back if he had gone away in the way he described? Probably not, I expect, as to me this would show a total lack of respect for me and my feelings, and also it would reflect what it was he really wanted out of life which, as I had thought such a long time ago, seemed to be much more than just me and all that I could offer.

So, we reached a bit of a stalemate. I couldn't say to him that I was happy about what he wanted and he couldn't say he didn't want it. Well, at least we were both being honest, which was better than not.

The mood went quieter as the night went on. Marc stayed over and I didn't sleep too well as the night hadn't gone the way I had expected it to, and also I wasn't feeling too great about myself again, so I was constantly mulling things over in my mind.

The next morning was quiet as well; we didn't get out of bed until 8.50 a.m. and he had breakfast and left the house. We didn't part on bad terms, though.

That night, on the phone, I asked him if he had booked his trip yet. He told me that he wasn't going to because of all the issues it would bring. At that stage, I just hoped that if we did get back together, he wouldn't then feel bitter about it – feeling as though I was standing in the way of him getting what he wanted out of life. I should have said this to him at the time. We ended the call by agreeing that he would come back on Thursday night so we could chat more about it all.

That day, I made some phone calls about the baby, most notably to a firm of solicitors in England to see if they knew of any support networks for gay men who have gone through a surrogacy process. The lawyer I spoke to had actually gone through surrogacy herself with her female partner to have a child, and was very helpful indeed. She confirmed that there was no network that she knew of, and that they were thinking of setting one up. She took my contact details for the future, just in case they wanted to let me know what they were doing. I had a really good chat with her and was telling her about the issues we were having with the hospital. She was very understanding and supportive, and I was kind of wishing that we had used her services instead of the lawyer I had used. But that would have been impossible, as I needed to use a lawyer based in Scotland.

More Issues ...

On Thursday 29 July, I missed a call from Kerry early on, so I called her back as soon as I noticed it. She had called to let me know that she had phoned the hospital and they were seemingly no further forward, except that they had referred the matter to their legal department and to their Social Services team. This had caused her to worry, so I tried to deal with her fears. She said she didn't want social workers in her life and I explained that it would be me and Marc they were looking at and not her, which seemed to appease her a bit. She also reiterated the fact that she didn't want a baby in her life and that if she did, she would have had one with her husband.

I suggested that I call the hospital to see if we could arrange for some sort of meeting, and her response was quite surprising. She said that she didn't want me to as she felt as if we were taking over. She said that the last time we met, she felt like she had just been pushed out of the way and Marc and I were running things. This was when I was having my blood taken and we were all talking to the midwife about the plan that we needed to create. We certainly hadn't pushed her out of the way. When we had gone into that room, I had to sit next to the midwife while she took my blood. Kerry had gone to sit on the bed behind her, so Marc sat in the chair next to me. Physically, we hadn't pushed her out of the way. When we were having the conversation about the plan, at some point the midwife's back was facing Kerry, but there was nothing I could do about that. Also, Marc and I were making it clear to the midwife what we wanted, which of course we were right to do. I know that Kerry was carrying the baby, but the issues we were discussing were about the baby itself, and how it was going to be handed to us –

nothing to do with any of Kerry's health or medical conditions.

I did apologise to her for the fact that we seemed to have made her feel that way, and she seemed to calm down a bit. We just about ended the call after that point, as there wasn't much else to talk about, and it made me feel crap – again!

Straight after this, I called our lawyer to explain that we were having issues with the hospital. I asked him if he knew of other hospitals who had overseen the birth of a child when it was being handed to surrogate parents, and he told me that Ninewells Hospital in Dundee had done one. He also said he would speak to his colleague to see if she knew of any. I sent Kerry a quick text to let her know about this, but I didn't get any response. She certainly knew how to make someone feel really bad. I then called Marc to let him know what had happened. He had a more sensible view – it was probably just her hormones playing up or something.

So, that was that – yet another issue. I really wished Kerry would contact one of these surrogacy support groups, like SurrogacyUK.org, so at least she could have got some practical advice and moral support from someone who had either been through the process, or at least understood it a lot more than we did.

Marc was round again that night and we chatted some more about getting back together, as well as doing the gardening, having tea, walking the dog together and going shopping for food and such like. It was a nice night, but we didn't get much further forward. What we did manage to achieve was booking a weekend away in Glasgow the following weekend for our birthdays and also agreeing where we wanted to go on holiday. We finally agreed that Mykonos was ideal, so we picked a hotel and looked on three different websites to find the best price.

Birthdays

The weekend of 7 August, Marc and I went over to Glasgow for our birthday weekend – and it was great. We were booked into the Thistle Hotel on Cambridge Street and when we arrived, we found that we had been upgraded to a suite, rather than just a double room, and it was just a great place. It was double the size of a normal hotel bedroom, but also had an enormous comfy lounge.

That weekend we did some shopping, went out for drinks, got drunk, had a dance and a walk and some good chats, and I really enjoyed myself. It was a shame it all had to end, but it was good spending time with Marc without having to get involved with all the usual chores, or walking the dog, etc.

We came home on the Monday, which was our actual birthday, and just had a quiet night in with some wine and telly. We just chatted about things in general, as well as about getting back together and moving in to Liddesdale Place together again (this was the first flat I ever lived in when I moved to Edinburgh, which I had since bought from my previous landlord and rented out). It was down to earth with a bump after my long weekend, though, as I had to go back to work on the Tuesday and had lots and lots of work to do.

That day, I sent an email to Kerry as I hadn't heard from her since the last stroppy call she had made to me. I had emailed about the support offered by Surrogacy UK, and it was meant to be a nice friendly supportive and caring email, but I didn't get a reply. My intentions were good – I was trying to help Kerry find some support for herself in going through this whole process, and had done some digging around before I emailed her. I've included the text of my email below, the reasons for which will become apparent later on.

Hi Kerry,

How are you doing? It was both our birthdays yesterday, so we ended up in Glasgow on Sunday and had a night in the Polo Lounge. Most of yesterday was spent recovering from a hangover!

I wanted to let you know that we managed to make contact last week with a couple of guys who are going through surrogacy down south, and they have suggested we all join surrogacyuk.org. They have a large network of people who have done this before, although people generally join them because they are looking for a surrogate, or want to be a surrogate mum. They did say we might be able to join for free, as obviously we are not looking to get anything out of it other than some support.

They also said that they have a lot of women who have had a number of babies for other couples, and who know the process very well, and would happily talk to us all if we had any questions. I mentioned the thing about the hospital and what they said was that most surrogate mums put what they want to happen in writing to the hospital, and ask for a written confirmation from the hospital that they agree to it. They don't know of anywhere where it's been an issue before, although they did say that it should always come from the surrogate mum.

They did say that they know of one case where the baby was born in Glasgow; they just didn't know which hospital.

It'd be good to have a chat soon and a catch up. Let me know when you are around?

Dave

Later that night, I sent Kerry a text to say I had emailed and hoped she was okay, but yet again there was no response.

This really did make me feel very uncomfortable, but I didn't know what I could do about it. I decided I would just give her a ring at the end of the week if I didn't hear back from her. In the meantime, I'd just keep myself busy at work and hoped I wouldn't worry or panic too much.

By Friday of that week, I still hadn't heard a thing, so I thought I would wait until later that day to get in touch and see what had happened. Whatever was the matter with her, I wasn't going to give her the opportunity to complain that I wasn't making an effort.

As planned, I called her on the Friday, at lunchtime. She answered and said she was driving so she couldn't talk. I politely asked if I should ring her later on and she told me that I should text first as she was really busy just now, which I agreed I would do, and we said goodbye. I came off the phone feeling very deflated and concerned yet again. I had no idea how she was, what was happening with the baby, if she had heard from the hospital or whether she herself was fit and well. By the looks of her Facebook pages, she was obviously keeping well and it looked as if she had been in Edinburgh earlier in the week, as there were some new pictures on there of her and her family at Edinburgh Castle. All quite bizarre!

I decided I would leave it until after work to drop her a quick text, tell her I was free and leave the ball in her court, so to speak.

Women

That evening, once I was indoors, I sent Kerry the quick text telling her I was free. After about half an hour, I received a response, by text, which read:

> *To be honest with you, I would rather just get back in contact when your child is on the way. I already explained how you made me feel the day you and Marc were at the hospital then you carried on to send the email telling me we should join some internet group. You and Marc can do what you want but please don't tell me what to do. I thought with explaining how you made me feel you would have backed off, but obviously not.*

I was absolutely gutted and couldn't quite believe what she had said, or that she had said it by text. It really did show a certain low level of maturity that you wouldn't expect from someone who had agreed to go through a surrogacy process. It made me wonder if she really could cope with this whole thing. If she reacted like this after an issue she had with a ten-minute discussion at the hospital, and couldn't even find it in herself to want to resolve it, then what the hell was she doing going through this whole process at all?

I wanted to reply and even started to write a text back to her, but after discussing it with Marc, we decided against it for a while. It did ruin my night, though, and instilled a sense of panic in me about the whole thing going wrong. I really didn't know what to do next. I thought about calling Emma to see if there was anything she could do, but then thought that would probably go down like a lead balloon with Kerry, so decided just to leave it and maybe send a response next week.

This also raised the question of how we were supposed to find out what was going to happen at the hospital on the day of the birth. As far as we knew, no plan had been agreed and we didn't know at this stage what progress was being made with the arrangements.

Kerry was due to be back at the hospital for a scan in a couple of weeks' time, and she would apparently find out the baby's sex for sure that day. Maybe she would just get in touch of her own free will when that happened. Who knew? She must be the most unpredictable, hot-headed, argumentative person I have ever met and I couldn't wait for this all to be over.

On the Monday night, after all of this had happened, I decided to call Emma and just let off some steam. I explained everything and thankfully, Emma understood. She told me that she had called Kerry the previous week just for a chat, but she hadn't answered. So, she left Kerry a message saying hello and just to call back if there was anything she wanted to talk about. Kerry hadn't called her back. After some lengthy discussion, Emma said she would call Kerry at the end of the week, but wouldn't say that she had spoken to me. She would ring me first to let me know when she was going to call and I would tell Emma if I had heard anything at that point. I expect it would make things worse if Kerry thought I had gone to Emma telling tales.

On a positive note, that day, Marc had called to tell me that Carol, Rebecca's mum, had bought some things for the baby from Asda, as there was a sale on baby things. We agreed that we would go and have a look the next day.

On the Friday of that week, Emma called Kerry and managed to speak to her. When she called me to let me know, she assured me that everything was fine, but she repeated what Kerry had said to me: that we were talking over her in the hospital on the day of the scan. This wasn't something I recalled at all. But, there was no point in arguing. Kerry said to Emma that she would of course keep us informed of progress as we moved through the next weeks, and would also let me know the outcome of the scan the following week. There was no talk of us actually speaking to her, though, and Emma said she was going to talk to Kerry the following week to check how she was feeling. This made me feel slightly better, although not 100%. At least I knew she was alive and well, and that things were okay as far as the baby was concerned.

Scare Tactics?

On Sunday 22 August, out of the blue, I received a worrying text from Kerry, which led to an even more worrying text exchange, the exact details of which were as follows:

Kerry: Could you find out from your lawyer if it still takes six weeks to get a parental order in place if the baby is born early? Thanks.

Me: Hi. It can only be applied for as soon as the baby is six weeks old. Hope all is well. D.

Kerry: Can you clarify something else please? Been having a look over contract and solicitor's agreement. What would happen if baby was born premature and didn't make it (GOD FORBID). Have to ask as there is nothing down in any of them?

Me: We'd need to check with Emma. I'll speak to her tomorrow.

Kerry: That would be a good idea as I would like to know where I stand in all likely situations!

After this, all sorts of thoughts entered my head. I was envisaging some sort of scenario where Kerry was trying to force the baby out before she went on holiday (at the end of September) and obviously this would pose a risk to the baby's health. I was sure even she wouldn't stoop this low, but giving her frame of mind over the past few weeks, God only knew what she could do.

Marc was quite supportive about this and managed to

keep a level head, which kept me fairly calm. We agreed that I would call Emma the next day and talk this through with her, and then ask her to ring Kerry to explain things to her. There would have been no point in me trying to call Kerry at all.

On Monday 23 August, I just nipped onto Facebook to see what was happening, to find that Kerry had now removed me as a friend. Not really a shock I suppose, but very odd yet again as she was one of the people who asked me to join in the first place.

I spoke to Emma later that morning, talked her through the text exchange I had with Kerry the day before and explained my concerns about the flight, etc. Emma was very understanding and agreed to phone Kerry later that day to answer her questions; if the baby was stillborn, or didn't survive until the parental order process, there was no provision for payment in her contract. I didn't think it would be appropriate for me to let Kerry know this, as I could just imagine another whole barrage of texts complaining that I'd done something else she was not happy about, or that she wouldn't have agreed to this if she had known.

Kerry had told me some time earlier that she wasn't in this for the money, and that the payment was just a bonus; she just wanted to be able to help out a couple who couldn't have children for themselves. I was starting to think that she had told me a bit of a porky when she said this. I had always accepted that for most women, acting as a surrogate was in some way about financial as well as personal reward. I suppose I just hadn't expected it to come across as coldly as this when it finally emerged.

Emma told me that when she and Kerry had spoken the week before, she asked how everything was health-wise, and Kerry had said it was all great; in fact, this was the best pregnancy she had ever had compared to the others. That really took me aback.

After my conversation, I looked up the whole issue about pregnant women flying and it turned out that she should be okay; the general rule seems to be that they can fly up to about thirty-five weeks or so. In this case, Kerry should have been at about thirty-four when she returned from Puerto Rico.

I dreaded waiting for 5.00 p.m. to see what the outcome of Emma's call was, but again it was out of my control. More waiting!

That afternoon, at about 2.30 p.m., Kerry texted me again, asking if I had asked Emma about her question. I told her that I had and that Emma was going to call her that afternoon, and I left it at that. I didn't want to get into another disturbing or distressing text conversation with her.

I was in meetings all afternoon, and when I came out at 5.30 p.m., I noticed that I had one missed call from Kerry and two texts, which read as follows:

Haven't heard anything from Emma, and her phone is going straight to answer phone. Would appreciate it if u could tell me what she said when u spoke with her?

And then, five minutes later …

Ok, can't get any information from you or Emma and as I want to know where I stand, I've contacted solicitors!

I tried to ring her back, but she diverted my call, so I texted back and explained that I was just out of a meeting. I called Emma and her phone went straight to voicemail, so that was me stuck. What the hell could I do now?

A little later, a voicemail came through from Emma, saying she had spoken to Kerry and that everything was fine; the baby was kicking like mad and there were no problems at all. This just didn't make sense to me whatsoever! Emma also said in her message that Kerry had called my lawyer and that I might want to speak to him when I get the chance. I couldn't call Emma back as seemingly her mobile was out of order.

That night was such a miserable one; I sat indoors, by myself, and cried. The pills I was taking to help me stop smoking seem to be making me so down that I was thinking about coming off them. Even though I was down to half dose, I couldn't help thinking they were making me react in the way I was doing, and it was doing me no favours, apart from that I wasn't smoking.

The next morning, I spoke to my lawyer. He told me Kerry had left a message with his secretary where she had said she believed the baby was either going to be stillborn or have a disability, and she wanted to know where she stood legally. I explained to the lawyer what had been going on recently and also that I believed that Kerry thought she had made a mistake in getting involved in all of this. He agreed to call her back and let me know later on what had been said. All I was bothered about was why she believed something was wrong, and I asked the lawyer to try and find out for me. It was odd that the next scan was due just two days after this, so I had no idea why Kerry was thinking this way. It was all just too upsetting for words.

I tried to get in touch with Emma again, both on her mobile and also on the office number I found for Surrogate Pathways on the internet, but didn't manage to get hold of her at all.

Later that morning, I went outside to vent yet more frustration and called Marc as I just needed to talk. After a few minutes of chatting, Emma called and I vented all of my frustration with her. I explained what my lawyer had told me and she said it sounded like there has been a mix up with what Kerry had said. Emma reiterated that Kerry had confirmed that all was well with the baby; it was kicking like mad and all was fine, except that she had a minor water infection, which she was off to see the doctor about. She had also said to Emma that she was looking forward to the scan on Thursday, and that she knew we were looking forward to finding out about the sex of the baby so we could start shopping for him or her.

This all just sounded so confusing and frustrating. On the one hand, Kerry was being positive and upbeat with Emma and on the other, she was refusing to talk to me at all. I just couldn't work it all out. I ended up really going off on one with Emma, in particular about Kerry's behaviour towards me, the language she used in her text messages and her impatience in getting the answers she was looking for. I explained to Emma how this really was making me feel and I just wanted Kerry to understand that. Emma told me that she would speak to her again that afternoon and see if she could explore any more of the reasoning behind it.

After that call, I also called Marc again and couldn't stop ranting, to the point that he had to tell me to calm down. I knew getting myself all worked up about this wasn't helping anyone, but I just felt so out of control that I couldn't help myself. I think I also decided that if my general mood wasn't better by the following weekend, I was going to come off the Champix, as it really didn't seem to be doing me any good at all.

Emma called me back again at lunchtime to let me know she had spoken to Kerry again and that Kerry had had her conversation with the lawyer. She said Kerry was now perfectly happy about everything, but that she still didn't want to speak to me. Emma explained that the way we made her feel in the hospital, coupled with the email I had sent her about Surrogacy UK, had left her very angry. Emma said maybe we might be able to speak again in a few weeks. It didn't leave me feeling that much better, but at least there were no issues to resolve at this stage.

Just after 3.00 p.m. on that day, I received an email from the lawyer, explaining his conversation with Kerry. Here's what it said:

Dear David,

I refer to our conversation this morning. I spoke to Kerry early this afternoon. She asked me what the situation with regards to reimbursement of expenses would be if the child was born with difficulties, or indeed, very unfortunately, died prior to birth, at birth or shortly thereafter.

I directed her to clause fourteen of the agreement, which I think is clear. My interpretation of that clause is that in the event of such an unfortunate event as the death of the child as described above, Kerry would be entitled to receive reimbursement of her reasonable costs and expenses arising from the matters described in clause fourteen.

I am confident that that is the position.

I found it rather an odd question, and she did appear somewhat excitable during my telephone conversation with her. I reassure you that the above comprises the extent of my conversation, simply advising her on my interpretation of the agreement she entered into. As I explained, I cannot offer her any advice, as I act for you and Marc, and to do so would constitute a conflict of interest.

Please let me know if you have any further concerns.

I was glad at least that someone else found her attitude excitable! Hopefully, that had put the matter at rest, at least for a while.

On Thursday 26 August, I was going to find out about the sex of the baby. I'd managed to put the whole thing to the back of my mind as far as I could, but that wasn't going to be possible today. Emma thought that the scan was at about 11.00 a.m., so I had made sure I didn't have any meetings which could conflict with a small chance of some excitement. I was full of a cold that morning, so wasn't feeling the best, and could have done with something to cheer me up.

By 10.45 a.m. I was way too nervous and excited, even more so than the way I felt on the day of the twenty-week scan. I just kept checking my phone to see if any texts had come through. I hoped to God that Kerry was actually going to let me know.

It's a ...

... baby that refuses to reveal its sex! How bloody annoying!

At 12.15 p.m., as I was sat having lunch with Melanie from work, a text came through from Kerry which said that the baby wouldn't open its legs, so again they couldn't tell what the sex was. I sent back a polite, neutral response and left it at that. I also sent a text to the family, and to Marc, to let them know.

Emma called me at 12.30 p.m. as she had just spoken to Kerry, and told me that everything was fine with the baby and with Kerry. Also, the hospital had seemingly agreed to provide Marc and me with a separate room and when the baby was born, they were going to bring it into us straight away. They were going to confirm all this with Kerry when she was back there in four weeks' time. So, I suppose, that was one worry over.

There was nothing much else to say or report, but at least I knew all was okay and that did make me feel much better, especially in light of the message Kerry had left at the lawyers earlier in the week.

Marc and Me, Again

On that day, Thursday 26 August, Marc moved back into the house. It still felt as if we had a lot to talk about, but the plan for the first weekend in September was for us to start moving into the flat at Liddesdale Place, as it would feel wrong for us both to be moving from different places into the one. So, that was that – we were back together. It all seemed to happen very silently, however, and not with any sense of excitement or happiness whatsoever. It felt a bit – well, very – surreal.

The weekend was quite an odd one. I should have been feeling pleased about us being back together and making a go of it, but to be honest, it didn't feel anything remotely like that at all. Marc was very distant and I felt as though he was regretting ever having said he would come back, and that he wanted to be with me. I was trying to be fun and keep us busy, but it still didn't seem to work too well at all. I could only wait and see really, but things were still going to have to improve for this to work out.

On the Saturday night, I was trying to get all excited about the whole thing again, so I went onto Facebook and did the thing where you say that you are in a relationship with someone. At the point, Marc saw what I'd done (Facebook sent him an automatic email message to let him know) and he seemed to be absolutely mortified. His reaction of 'What have you gone and done that for?' really knocked me for six, to the point where I just felt like such a fool.

Although I tried my best to deal with it so it didn't spoil the rest of the night, I just couldn't. It was the oddest response to a statement of what I thought was fact that I had ever seen in my life. It just made me feel so insecure that I was probably speechless for the next hour or so. If this was the shape of things to come, I'd have expected us to last about another month before we fell apart again. But, I had to get on with my weekend and try to put this and the potential reasons for it to the back of my mind. That was a very difficult one indeed.

By the Sunday night, after a busy weekend packing, eating, walking the dog and various other practical things, it was time for a good sleep. There was no change in terms of Marc's attitude towards me, no advances towards me being made by him and no attempt at trying to make me feel good about us making a go of it again. I wondered then if I had made the right choice in letting him back into my life like this, or whether we really should have just waited a while longer to see what else might have happened. I know what would have happened for me, as there were a number of opportunities I could have taken up to see where they might have led, and some of them I knew may have been good, but I tried to steer myself clear of those ones for as long as I could without making too many embarrassing excuses about why I couldn't meet/speak/get in touch with them. At that stage, I was guessing I'd never know if any of them might have worked out.

All I could do now was just make the effort needed on my part to support a relationship with Marc, and that was that. Whether he reciprocated was a choice he had to make, but I did wonder now if that would ever happen, or if him wanting to come back was a response to his fear of knowing I was capable of making a go of it with someone else. It was just all too complicated. Even by the end of the working day on Monday, I wasn't feeling too positive at all about it. I tried that night to talk to him about my fears and anxieties, though I'm not sure if it got me anywhere.

The following day, Tuesday, was a more positive one; I went to have a look round the university's nursery facility on Dalkeith Road, where I was given a guided tour by a very pleasant woman. Actually, it was a really nice experience; the nursery was based in two old detached houses with lovely gardens and was obviously a very professional one. There must have been about twenty kids there at least, all looking like they were thoroughly enjoying themselves – nobody screaming or looking like they were about to burst into tears – and the only issue I had was the smell of poo in one of the rooms where the youngest kiddies were. It wasn't too offensive, though.

I left there feeling very positive about it all. I wasn't sure if that was the place I would be using, as it was the wrong side of work, but at least I knew now what to expect. I still had to find a few other places, hopefully based in Stockbridge, where I was about to move.

The rest of the week was taken up by packing and sorting the house out in advance of the move. Thankfully, I only had to work until the Thursday, as from 6.00 p.m. that day it was all systems go! I was actually looking forward to the move at that stage, plus things had seemed to improve somewhat with Marc and me by that point as well, which put me in a better frame of mind about the whole move to the flat.

The move itself was pretty okay. We did have a few choice words when we were trying to organise things, do the painting, or lift furniture, but that was just bickering – nothing serious. In fact, we ended up working really well together; we managed to achieve loads in what was a really short space of time. After redecorating the whole flat, putting up new blinds, cleaning it and Marc putting an alarm in, we eventually moved most of our things in on Monday 6 September. However, it was at that point that we both started to wonder if we really had done the right thing; it really was so much smaller than the four-bedroom house we were leaving. By the end of the night, though, we had most things in their rightful places and the dog had now moved in as well. We talked about how the hell a baby was going to fit in as well, but there was no point worrying about it at that stage. It would all work itself out in the end.

I actually had a great night's sleep that first night; my new blackout blinds were just great and it was so nice to be in such a quiet spot, without daylight flooding the bedroom at some ridiculously early time of day, as it did in the last place.

The next day was spent moving most of the rest of our things into storage. This wasn't anywhere near as enjoyable as the day before. We immediately increased the size of the storage we booked up to 85 square feet and even that didn't seem big enough. I was sure we would squeeze everything in, though.

Later that day, Kerry called. I didn't get to the phone in time, so I ended up having to call her back. My heart was racing, wondering what she was phoning for and my immediate reaction was to think the worst, so I just phoned her straight back to get it over with. She answered straight away and was fairly pleasant with me, chatting about ours and her holidays and things. She had originally phoned to tell me that she had met with people at the hospital, including social workers, and now they wanted to come and see me and Marc. So, she was warning us that someone was going to get in touch. She then explained that she was already in contact with these social workers for pre-existing issues. She also said that they had been concerned because of her postnatal depression, which she had after the birth of her youngest child. She had never told us this before. Neither had she told us that she already had social workers in her life – it wasn't too long ago that she told me she was worried about social work being involved in this child's birth, as she didn't want social workers in her life at all. I was suspecting a bit of a cover-up here.

As we talked further, we started to chat about the involvement of the lawyer the other week. She explained that she had started to have Braxton Hicks contractions and she wouldn't normally get these until about thirty-two weeks. She said she had also had a 'show', which meant that part of the mucus plug had come away. I had a bit of a panic, thinking this meant that the baby was going to come early, but she was adamant that it was going to stay in there until she had had her holiday! She then told me that this was the whole reason she had called the lawyer in the first place. She went on to mention how angry she was that the message I had been given by the lawyer was the wrong one – that the baby was either going to be stillborn or have a disability. Although I didn't say much to her about this, I did ask her to think how it had made us feel at the time.

So, all in all, it was an okay conversation. I agreed to let her know once the social workers had been in touch, and that was that. Thankfully, my heart slowed down.

On the Wednesday, the social workers called me to arrange a visit. That was booked for 6.00 p.m. the following Tuesday. They were going to come to the flat (two women called Kathleen and Andrea, I think). I wasn't worried about them coming, but I wasn't sure whether I should be or not to be honest. After what Kerry had said, I imagined it was all going to be just part of a process. At least I hoped it was.

That Friday, I did some research on Braxton Hicks and reassured myself that it wasn't the start of labour. Seemingly, these things can start from about seven weeks and the severity can range from mild to sometimes painful. Phew!

I didn't think too much about any of this over the weekend, as I had far too much to do; I was busy cleaning the old house and taking things to storage. In fact, I was absolutely shattered. When Marc got back from Aberdeen that Sunday, I was ready for my bed. He had taken the dog up there for the following three weeks to stay with his daughter and her mum, to save us having to put her in kennels while we were away on holiday in Mykonos.

That next week was a pretty busy one as well. Our plan

was to drive to Manchester on the Thursday night and stay in a hotel there, before catching the 8.00 a.m. flight the next day. Before then, we had lots to do: finalising the cleaning at the house at Clermiston Road, squeezing anything that was left into storage, getting our holiday clothes sorted out, sorting out finances, getting to work and so on. This was also the week when Dad was in hospital with a blocked artery in his leg. There was just too much going on. The issue with Dad got worse that week and by the Tuesday, he had been operated on three times. The family was in a tizz and I felt pretty helpless as I was stuck in Edinburgh and had the appointment with the social workers that night to look forward to.

The Visit from the Social

At 6.00 p.m. on Tuesday 14 September, Andrea and Kathleen from the Glasgow Social Work team arrived, and I was glad they did. They were really nice people and explained initially why they were there. Seemingly, Kerry had had Social Services in her life for quite some. They didn't explain why and we didn't want to know. However, in view of this, they had taken a close interest in the surrogacy issue.

When Kerry decided to use the Southern General Hospital rather than her usual hospital for managing the pregnancy and birth, it was possibly because she thought that they would use a different set of social workers than her usual ones and therefore, this wouldn't be picked up on. However, when the Southern informed their social work team, Kerry's usual team were informed automatically. This then led to what was classed as a child protection meeting. Sounds scary! In view of all this, the social workers agreed they needed to meet with Marc and me to check us out and ensure that we were responsible, intelligent people; hence their visit.

We chatted in general about the surrogacy and then got onto our relationship with Kerry. To my absolute relief, it turned out that the social workers knew exactly what Kerry was like and basically pointed out that our experiences of her were exactly the same as everyone else's. She is fiery, temperamental, not as mature as she makes out and can be very unreasonable. She is also a control freak who can fly off the handle at the smallest issue. In fact, the social workers were used to being thrown out of her house. This was such a relief to hear. They told us that her behaviour was not our fault; it was just the way she always was. I was so pleased to hear that I hadn't in fact done anything wrong at all. Marc and

117

I were both very talkative and I was really pleased to see him taking such an active part in the conversation.

After the main part of our business was over, Kathleen asked to have a look around the flat, so I gave her a whirlwind tour of the four small rooms we had and we chatted as we went. Then, before they left, I explained that Kerry had asked me to call her to let her know how it went. I checked on what I should say and we all agreed that I should confirm that they were just ensuring we were decent people.

After they had gone, I called Kerry to let her know and my heart was racing as usual. She was in good spirits, thankfully, so I explained that the visit had gone well, that the social workers seemed really nice and that they were just asking about who we were, what we did and our relationship – all straightforward. Kerry was obviously in a chatty mood, so we talked about our forthcoming holidays and how much we were looking forward to them. She told me that she had had contractions since 3.00 p.m. that day, and was about to go and have a bath to see if they would settle down. We were still at the twenty-nine-week stage, so I told her to make sure it stayed in for at least another few weeks. I really didn't fancy the thought of it being born when we were away, or when she was away for that matter.

We ended the conversation on pleasant terms. I was relieved and in a much more positive mood yet again.

That night, Mum called me to let me know that Dad's left leg was going to be amputated if the third operation didn't work. It didn't sound positive at all and the next day, my fears were confirmed. The hospital had decided to amputate and it would be done on Thursday 16 September. I felt awful and had a real dilemma on my hands. I was due to fly to Mykonos on the Friday, for my first real holiday in over five years, and I had thought that this really was going to be my last chance for a holiday like this for a long, long time. Should I or shouldn't I go?

I spoke to loads of people about it and by the end of my working day on the Wednesday, I had decided I should go. This was mainly due to that fact that I could see Dad on the Thursday, either before or after his operation, and as long as it had gone to plan, he would be in hospital for some time afterwards. Even if I cancelled my holiday, all I would be able to do for him would be visit every now and again, which would be a bit daft. I could keep in touch with the family by phone, they could call me if there was an emergency and I would see him when I flew back on 1 October. So, as far as I was concerned, I didn't feel like I shouldn't go away. I just felt very selfish about it.

Marc and I drove down south on the Thursday and I went to see Dad with the family. It was a very upsetting experience; his left leg had been amputated above the knee and he was in a very confused state, talking but not really making much sense, and falling in and out of sleep. I stayed there for a couple of hours and saw him twice, which I was glad about, although I did get upset when I was leaving them all.

That night, Marc and I stayed in a hotel near Manchester Airport and flew out the next morning for a fantastic holiday; and it was just that – absolutely fantastic. We had a few fall-outs, and our relationship changed quite a bit for the better as a result, but it was just great. We talked, laughed, drank, met some nice folk, relaxed and generally had the best time ever. However, always at the back of my mind were Kerry and the baby, wondering if she was going to make her holiday and if she did, were we going to get a call saying we needed to go to Spain as she had gone into labour? Thankfully, that didn't happen, though she did text asking about whether her money was going to get paid that month, which of course it was, on payday. I sent her a text wishing her a good holiday, but unsurprisingly she didn't respond.

119

I felt so good after the holiday and was pleased that we had gone. When we finally got back, we went to see Dad at home; he was doing a lot better and was now in a wheelchair, but at least he was talking and was more like the dad I knew before his operation, which was a relief. Sadly, we didn't stay too long; we had to head home by 9.30 p.m. So, we got indoors by about 1.15 a.m., both shattered and stayed up until 4.00 a.m. sorting out washing and stuff.

On the Saturday, we did more sorting out and headed to Aberdeen to pick up the dog and see Rebecca and her mum. It turned out that they had bought loads of stuff for the baby, which was great. I was taken a bit by surprise by the extent of the things they had bought and nearly panicked thinking about where it would all go. I was really grateful, though. We could only take some of it home, as we couldn't think where we could put it all yet – there was still loads of sorting out to do.

That night, we were home again by 11.30 p.m. or so, both shattered again. Marc had gone all quiet, although he said he was just tired, which I hoped was the case. We sat up for a while and must have passed out at about 2.00 a.m.

Sunday was yet another day of sorting things out and then, that night, we managed to have a good soak in the bath and got to bed at a reasonable hour. The next day was to mark the start of the final stretch before the baby was due: a few more weeks at work and loads of things to buy, including pram, car seat and a whole load of other stuff, but this was it – only about seven weeks to go if she went full term. Gulp!

The Final Stretch?

On Tuesday 5 October, Kerry called me when I was at work. As usual, as soon as I saw her name appear on my phone, my heart started to race like mad. But there was no need to panic – well, not really anyway. She was back from holiday and had had a great time. She told me she had a great tan, but also that she was rushed into hospital the Friday before she went away with a suspected blood clot to her lungs. Sometimes I struggled to believe these things. Anyhow, all was fine now.

She mentioned the appointment she had on 23 September, where she didn't have a scan; they just measured her. She also said that she still thought it was a boy, so I was explaining that some of our relatives had been buying girls things, although I had told them it was not definite as yet. Then she told me that she had had two 'shows' whilst she was away, and also one at the airport when she got back yesterday, but again all was fine. She was still getting the Braxton Hicks contractions, but they weren't real ones, yet at least.

I asked her what had been agreed by the hospital and she said that the social workers have sorted everything out for us, which seemed great. I asked what exactly had been agreed and she told me that she wasn't sure at that stage, but was waiting for another appointment with the midwife, so it would all be explained to her then. She wasn't sure when this would be – hopefully soon.

The call ended in a rushed way as she had another call coming through, but at least it was all fairly positive. I was glad she hadn't called when we were away, as that would have ruined my holiday and I was also glad she had made it back to the UK in one piece, and with the baby still intact. Another panic over!

There were a number of other questions I wanted to ask, but I didn't get the chance, such as what the plans were for the baby to be induced at thirty-seven weeks, as she had previously said would happen. As I didn't get the chance, I sent her a text saying how much I appreciated her call and also asking if we could chat again at the end of the week. I didn't hear back from her, which was no surprise.

That lunchtime, I called the social workers for a quick update and they were positive that all was going to work out well. They said they would be calling Kerry at some point soon for a catch up, but were positive nothing would go wrong. They were in talks with the midwives at the Southern General so that they could ensure that the baby was passed to us as soon as humanly possible.

That afternoon, I called the health visitor at my local GP practice to start the ball rolling there. I spoke to someone called Dawn, who basically explained that as soon as the baby was born we needed to call them and they would set the wheels in motion for them to visit and start the usual process. That all seemed a bit too easy, but then they didn't ask who we were and so had no idea it would be a male couple bringing up the baby. I know that this should have been nothing to worry about, but surrogacy in itself isn't the norm and surrogacy with a gay couple involved is even further from it.

The week after our holiday was a pretty busy one, sorting out clothes, more things in the flat, storage and other arrangements. We did try looking for prams and car seats and on the Saturday, we spent some time in Mothercare finding a travel system that would work for us. We managed to find one, which was way too expensive, and agreed that we would end up buying one from eBay, which would save us a fortune.

At the end of that week, I decided I would stop drinking until the baby was born (that makes me sound like an alcoholic, but really, I'm not!). My thinking was that if we were called and told that the baby was on its way, at least I would be sober enough to jump in the car and drive over to Glasgow. I couldn't bear it if the call came through from Kerry and I wasn't in a fit state to drive. I could always rely on Marc, but this was one thing I wanted to be able to do myself. So, on Sunday 10 October, we finished off what was left of a litre bottle of vodka and that was that – alcohol-free for quite some time to come. I did take some solace from the fact that it would help me lose weight and I would feel a lot healthier for a while to come.

False Alarm!

For the following week, all was pretty quiet. I sent a text to Kerry just to see how she was, but heard nothing back as usual. Then, on Sunday 17 October, while Marc and I were out walking the dog, a text came through from her saying,

> *Hi David. I thought I should let you know I'm in hospital in the labour suite. Been contracting for a couple of hours but not in labour. They are just keeping an eye on things cos I'm early. Aarrrggghhh!*

Well, there was nothing I could do; I wrote back asking her to keep us posted and she said she would, and the rest of the night I was pretty much on edge wondering what was going to happen.

The next morning I texted her again and she said she was still having contractions but there was no sign of labour. Then, at about 3.00 p.m., she called me. It turned out that she had been in the hospital since lunchtime on the Sunday, and had been having contractions every ten minutes, but her cervix wasn't open, so she definitely wasn't in labour. She told me that everything was okay as far as she knew and that she was going for a scan at 3.40 p.m. to check everything out. She would let me know if they found out the sex. She also explained that this was now having an effect on her relationship with her husband. She said she had been keeping him and everyone else at a distance; she had managed to detach herself from the baby and didn't want anyone else to be getting involved, so she had been keeping everyone at arm's length. When the staff at the hospital asked her if she wanted to talk to anyone, she had said she didn't, for that specific reason. I told her she could talk to us at any time if she wanted to, but I didn't get a response to that. I probably didn't expect one.

She also explained that when the baby was born, we would be allowed into the labour suite once her and the baby were cleaned up, so that we could have immediate contact to start the bonding process. This wasn't what we had expected, as we thought the baby was just going to be brought out of there and into whatever room we were put into. I was going to question her at that point, but I thought it might seem like I was trying to change what she had wanted, and there was no point at all in doing that.

Kerry had also explained that she was changing her consultant at the hospital and was going to see the new one on Wednesday to talk about the possibility of the baby being induced. So, for the next hour, I sat at work waiting and not able to concentrate on anything until I had heard from her. Then, at about 4.30 p.m., she sent a text saying, 'All measuring up fine. It's weighing just under 5lb. Still can't get a proper view, but think it's a girl.' And that was that. So, at least there was a bit of relief that everything was okay, although I was disappointed that it was just a text. She had said earlier that after the scan she was going home, so I just assumed all was okay from that point onwards.

When Marc and I discussed all this later on, he said he didn't want us to go into the labour suite and I agreed, although I did explain that we might not have any other choice. I agreed that I would contact the social workers that week to find out if there was anything we could do to change what Kerry had said, although I wasn't too hopeful about it.

The rest of that week was a pretty quiet one: just the usual mundane drudgery at work and taking it easy at home. However, we did go out and buy a few bits and bobs for the baby, including some vests and sleep suits, a towel and a glove puppet, which I found really funny.

On the Thursday, I called the social workers and spoke to

Andrea to see if she knew the outcome of Kerry's meeting with the new consultant from the day before. Andrea didn't even know that was happening, so she promised to chase it up for me by speaking to the midwives and calling me back later that day. Andrea told me that the hospital didn't believe what Kerry was saying about the baby having to be induced, meaning that there was no reason for the baby to be born early at all.

We did have a bit of a laugh at one stage. Andrea said that she bet we couldn't wait to have Kerry out of our lives, and I agreed. She also said we must have been relieved that the baby has no genetic link to Kerry, at which we laughed and I explained that I'd be giving it back if it did.

For probably the millionth time during this process, I started formulating the letter in my mind that I'd wanted to send to Emma, just explaining how awful this whole process had been. I couldn't help thinking in one respect that she really should have put Kerry through a proper vetting procedure before even contemplating arranging for us to meet. Granted, if that had been the case, we probably wouldn't have been expecting a baby to come along now, but some elements of the whole thing just seemed wrong. For a process that should have been so full of positivity and excitement, it had really been full of anxiety, stress, negativity and worry, and there really has been no enjoyment from it at all.

Looking back, the elements of this that had made me smile were few and far between; apart from that initial call when she told me she was pregnant and a limited number of conversations where she has been upbeat, it had all been horrendous. The major good points had been the interactions I had had with people when talking about the baby – family, friends and colleagues – but there should have been so much more.

However, I concede that a vetting procedure wouldn't

have told us what we really needed to know about Kerry, but it would have been good to have at least gone through that. Kerry is smart and would have made sure that nobody picked up on the fact that social workers were already in her life, for whatever reason. I also doubt if anyone could have really expected her personality to turn out the way it had, and I expect this could only really have raised its head if we had a lot more time to get to know her before the IVF process actually took place. Hindsight is a wonderful thing!

Yet More Drama

On Monday 25 October, I had a call from Kerry while I was at work. This time, she had yet more tales to tell. Seemingly, her husband had left her; she told me that he had run her off the road, that he had been seeing some 'slut' and that he had emptied out their bank account, as well as taking all the food out of their fridge. She told me that he blamed the pregnancy for it all and that her mum had to come round to fill her fridge with food. I really didn't know what to think – was she telling the truth, or was this a ploy to see if she could get some money out of us earlier than it was due?

As was usual when she phoned up to complain about something, I was supportive, told her how sorry I was and that if there was anything we could do, she just needed to ask. However, she told me that there was nothing anyone could do.

On the back of all of this, she told me that she had been to get checked out at the hospital and everything was fine, although she was told that she was 2 cm dilated. This basically meant that the baby could be born early, but similarly it could still be another four weeks, so I wasn't too concerned.

We ended the call on good terms, although I did then call the social workers to see if they could shed any light on what had gone on. I didn't hear back from them until Wednesday that week, but thankfully they knew everything and put my mind at rest. Kath told me that she had been in touch with Kerry on the Monday and had been told what had happened. She also contacted the police for more information about the car accident and had been reassured that it was exactly that.

I had another good chat with Kath about the whole situation and she assured me that everything was going according to plan. She had been in touch with the hospital and they had agreed for everything to happen the way we wanted it to. She was still 100% positive that there would be no issue in handing the baby over; Kerry really didn't want it for herself, so we really just had to make sure it all ran smoothly.

On the Thursday of that week, the midwife from the Southern General called to say she was helping to arrange parenting classes for us, and gave me the number for Linda, the lady who would run them. I managed to get in touch with Linda that afternoon and we were booked in for our class the following Thursday, 4 November at 2.00 p.m. I was grateful they had seen fit to arrange this, as I really was a novice at this whole thing. I was even more grateful that it was arranged just for us two; I couldn't bear the thought of being surrounded by straight folk and all the potential discrimination that could involve. Plus, with it being arranged for the following week, it meant it should have been in plenty of time before the baby was due to be born.

Parenting Class

So, the day of the class quickly came around and on 4 November, we were on our way to Glasgow where we were quickly met by Linda in the maternity wing of the Southern General. After being shown into what felt like a classroom (which I suppose was to be expected), Linda introduced herself and then oddly asked what we knew about what was going to happen the day the baby was born. So, I proceeded to explain what we had been told – that the baby would be handed to us immediately following birth; we would have a private room where we would look after him or her and then we'd be allowed home as any other new parents would be, as long as the baby was okay.

At this point, the day took a turn for the worse. Linda explained to us that there had been quite a bit of social work involvement in the past few days and now the agreed process was that once the baby was born, it would be taken straight to the special baby unit. This was where babies who were to be put up for adoption were taken, or where the mother was too ill to look after them. Then, there would need to be a child protection case conference to agree what would happen to the baby and then, and only then, we would be told what was going to happen. Also, we would only be allowed to take the baby home once my name was on the birth certificate. In the meantime, we could visit during visiting hours and that would be it.

Marc and I were both horrified. Yet again, this was something else to make the whole process seem negative and cold for us. Trying our best to keep calm, we asked Linda to bring Diane Paterson into the room; she was the 'lead' in this area and had been in contact with the social workers who had made all of these decisions.

Doreen, the original midwife we met weeks before, also came in to say hello and she was very supportive. She explained to us that she hadn't been sleeping because of this and she believed that it should all happen in the way we had wanted it to.

After a while, Diane came in. I didn't take to her from the moment she came into the room, although this was nothing personal – I'd decided I wouldn't like her even before I met her. She explained to us what Linda had already said, at which point Marc and I told her we believed that this was blatant discrimination on the basis of our sexuality. I tried to make the point that this wouldn't happen for any straight couple who were going through the same thing, and also that if the situation wasn't rectified, we would be bringing a claim for discrimination against the hospital. She tried her best to calm us down, but it didn't work. In the end, I suggested that she get hold of the social worker (it was Kathleen she had been dealing with) to clarify the exact situation.

So, Diane and Doreen left the room at this point. Linda then carried on trying to talk us through what we had originally intended to go there for. It wasn't the best session, although some of it was useful. I just wanted the other issues to be sorted out and only then would I be able to concentrate.

Diane came back into the room after a few minutes to tell us that she had spoken to Kathleen, and that Kathleen would call me to clarify the situation and – lo and behold – she did call a few minutes later. She explained to me that in view of the situation with Kerry and her own child protection issues, they had needed to be careful about how they managed the situation. However, so long as Kerry voluntarily gave up the child when it was born, the child would come straight to us. We would be given the same treatment any other new parents would get – our own space with the child – and we'd be allowed to go home with the baby at the same time as anyone else would. The only time that this wouldn't happen would be if Kerry refused to give up the baby. If this happened (and nobody expected it to), the child would be taken from Kerry and there would be a child protection case conference, which would determine what would happen to the baby. Kathleen said that the outcome of this would be that the child would come to us anyway, so it would just mean a delay to the process.

Our stance on all of this was that the baby should be put with us as soon as was practically possible, and Marc and I had made clear that we wouldn't accept it any other way. At least now it appeared as though things were resolved, so we could relax for the time being. So, we had the rest of our parenting class and learnt some useful things about cot death, feeding, bathing and interacting with the baby – and that was that.

I was pleased that Linda and Doreen had been so supportive and by the time we left, I felt nearly 100% reassured that all was going to go smoothly. It was a shame the same couldn't be said about our journey home, which took us the best part of four hours!

As soon as I could, the next morning, I called Kerry as I felt I should let her know what had happened. But, I first spoke to Diane to confirm that she had recorded what Kathleen had said, in writing, on Kerry's file, which she had. I also called Social Services and spoke to Susan (Kathleen's manager) to ask someone there to call Kerry to make sure she knew exactly what would be happening. I finally spoke to Kerry just before lunchtime; she told me that Kathleen had been in touch and confirmed exactly what she had told us. So, that was that – all resolved, everybody in the picture and everybody happy with it.

Kerry told me during the call that she was now living at her mum's, her husband had been stalking her and she thought the baby was going to arrive by the end of the weekend. I didn't know which part of that to believe, if any, so just agreed and listened. I just wanted it over with now; the sooner this was all done, and Kerry and her child protection issues were out of my life, the better.

OMG! It's Happening?

On Tuesday 9 November, what was supposed to be a normal day at work turned into one full of pressure. I was sitting in a meeting when I received a text from Kerry asking me to call. I'd presumed it wasn't anything urgent, but I nipped out to call her anyway. It took what felt like an eternity for her to answer, but when she did, she told me she had been into the hospital again that morning. She explained to the doctor in there that she was having emotional issues in coping with the pregnancy, especially because of what had been happening at home. So, they had finally agreed to arrange for the baby to be born early. That morning, she had been given a membrane sweep, which should induce labour. If it didn't work, she would be going into the hospital on Sunday at 10.00 p.m. and they would give her a pessary, which would definitely work and the baby would be born by Monday at the latest. I could hardly contain my excitement! That meant that within the space of six days, I would definitely be a dad. Oh my God!

Kerry sounded really pleased that it was going to be over with and I certainly was. She also said that the hospital had shown her the plan, which was going on her file, and everyone was happy with it. However, at the back of my mind was something telling me I should just check in with the hospital to confirm what Kerry had said, so I called and spoke to Diane Paterson, who confirmed that it was true. She also explained that the procedure that morning would work within twenty-four hours if it was going to. Otherwise, if the baby hasn't arrived by Sunday, they would induce her. She was really helpful and also confirmed the existence of the note on Kerry's file, which she agreed to email through to me.

I had to call Marc and he sounded almost as excited as me, which I was massively pleased about. I couldn't quite believe it still – just a few days to go and it would all be over, and all this hassle and stress would have disappeared. (I was also secretly pleased that some of the work meetings I had booked in for the next few days were going to be cancelled!)

My lunchtime that day was a mad dash home; I let the dog out, called Mum to tell her the news and dashed back to work to let my colleagues know. I was grinning from ear to ear for most of the day. The rest of the day passed pretty quickly, full of positive thoughts with the realisation of what was soon to happen. Though, as time went on, I started to think that maybe the baby was going to wait until it was properly induced before it came out.

That night, I sent Kerry a quick text asking how things were and she said she was having some cramps, but nothing else was happening.

On the Wednesday morning, I sent another and there was still no change. So, I was all set for the wait until the weekend. However, at 5.30 p.m., just as I got in from work, Kerry called sounding all excited. She told me she thought it was starting – labour, that is! She said her waters seemed to have broken and that she was constantly dribbling and having contractions every two minutes.

Me being me, I got all excited, thinking, 'What the hell do I do now?' She said that she was just sorting out the kids' stuff for school in the morning and then going to get her cousin, as it was her cousin that was going to the hospital with her. She said she didn't know when she was going to go to the hospital, but she didn't expect it would be too long. I asked her to let me know when she did, so that we could arrange to get there as well as soon as we needed to. Marc was home a few minutes after the call, so we chatted about what to do for the best and agreed we would just wait to hear from Kerry. We tried to carry on as normal for a while – had some toast, walked the dog, did some shopping at Boots, had tea – but I just couldn't settle. We also set up the new carrycot in the bedroom and Marc sorted out the sterilising unit for the bottles, so at least we were semi-prepared for when the baby came home. It was a bit weird putting all the bedding in the carrycot; as I was doing it, I was just thinking that the next time I looked into it, there may well be a baby in there!

All went quiet for a while after that. I sent Kerry a text just after 8.00 p.m. to see if there was any movement and she replied that her contractions were still every two minutes, though she had still not been seen by the doctors. I took that to mean that she was actually at the hospital, so I checked and she confirmed that she was. This disappointed me a bit, as I expected her to let me know when she was on her way. This was par for the course, I suppose, but still disappointing at such a late stage in the process.

I was sitting at home on the edge of my seat for the rest of the night and after a few texts, she let me know at 11.30 p.m. that the midwife had just checked her. She said that she wasn't dilated any more, so she wasn't in established labour. She'd been told it sounded like early labour, so she was told to go home and keep an eye on the contractions. So, that was that – a bit of a false alarm.

I'd kept the family informed throughout the evening about what had happened, so had to send them all a quick text to let them know. I think they were as disappointed as me.

We ended up staying up until 2.00 a.m. that night. I was overly excited and a bit disappointed to say the least. A few hours before, I was expecting that a baby was about to arrive and this whole process would be almost over.

Up at 7.30 a.m. the next day and there was no update from Kerry, so I took that to mean that there was no news. Once I got to work, I sent her a quick text asking if all was okay, but didn't receive a response. This put me on edge a bit, so at

9.00 a.m., I decided to call the hospital to see if I could find out anything.

There, I spoke to Diane Paterson and she didn't seem to know anything at all. I explained what had happened the night before and she explained to me that the waters breaking might be the waters at the back of the baby, rather than the main waters next to its head, but she did say that it sounded like Kerry would be going into labour pretty soon. I explained to Diane that I was concerned not to have heard from Kerry since the night before and was worried that she might have been in the hospital without us knowing about it. Diane then explained that it was down to Kerry to let me know if she was there and not her. I found this a bit odd, but didn't suppose I was in any sort of position to challenge her.

By 10.15 a.m., I still hadn't heard anything at all and my frustration got the better of me, so I decided I would call the social workers to see if they knew anything. I spoke to Kathleen Burns and explained the story of the past twenty-four hours; she wasn't aware of any of it at that stage. She told me that she had spoken to Kerry the day before about something different, but was happy to try and call her again. I asked Kathleen not to let Kerry know I had called her, as I didn't want any more bad feeling, so Kathleen confirmed that she would make the call on the pretence of picking up on something they discussed the day before. She agreed she would call me back as soon as she managed to make contact with Kerry, so yet again I was sitting about waiting at work.

By 11.00 a.m., it had been one of the slowest mornings of my life. For some reason, I'd expected the previous day to be my last one in the office until February – and this was before I'd heard about Kerry's waters breaking. I'd managed to get all of my little jobs done, had a handover with my manager and tied up some loose ends. So, I was now there with next to nothing to keep me occupied except writing this thing and going for the odd stroll around the building. My lack of patience was yet again doing my head in.

The closer it got to lunchtime, the more frustrated I became. I tried to call Kerry only to be met by her voicemail, so I ended up calling Diane Paterson again. I hadn't heard back from Kathleen, so didn't really know what else to do. Diane told me – in a way where she didn't want to be breaching patient confidentiality – that she believed I would find Kerry at home. So, at least she wasn't in hospital giving birth without me knowing about it. This did put my mind at rest for a while. I decided not to try contacting Kerry again for a few hours, as maybe she just wanted to be left alone for a while. Although it didn't really do me any favours, I certainly didn't want to rock the boat at this stage.

At 2.30 p.m., Kathleen called back. She hadn't managed to call Kerry, but she did get hold of the hospital. They had told her that Kerry's waters hadn't broken and that the plan was still the same: she would be taken into hospital on Sunday night and induced on Monday 15 November, the anniversary of Nanna's death in 1985 – not such a bad thing really.

Well, that was that for now and yet again, I was left feeling pretty deflated. I couldn't work out if Kerry was just being a little over dramatic the previous night or whether she just got it wrong. The absence of any contact from her by that stage in the day pointed me in the direction of the answer I believed to be right. Enough said.

That night was another quiet one; we went to Mothercare and bought a top and tail bowl – something I'd never heard of before, but it was what Marc had used when Rebecca was a baby. No contact from Kerry came through, but in one way that was a good thing.

The Friday of that week was going to be my last day at work for a few months and I started wondering how the whole process was going to work when Kerry went into hospital on the following Sunday night – how quick would it all be and when would the process to induce the baby actually start? So, I ended up ringing her, not really expecting her to answer, but she did. I asked how she was and she said she was pretty fed up with life. I reassured her that at least this would all be over in a couple of days and asked her what I intended to ask about the process. She explained that, as long as the labour ward wasn't too busy, she would be given the pessary to start labour between 8.00 p.m. and 10.00 p.m. on Sunday night, and then it should all start from there. We discussed how Marc and I were going to find out about labour starting, and whether we should make our way over on Sunday night and just wait around. Kerry said that her mum would keep us up to date with what was happening, and they would let us know as soon as it all started. I also asked her to let me know when she was heading to the hospital, so at least then we would know to be ready to leave at the point we needed to, and she agreed to do that.

Kerry then talked for a while about the situation with her and her husband. She told me that they had £30,000 worth of debts, but they were all in her name as he was blacklisted, so she was intending to go bankrupt and sell her house down south, seemingly a rental property, so that she could start that process. Tony hadn't apparently given her any money for her or the kids' upkeep, and she had contacted her lawyers and the CSA, but hadn't got anywhere yet. I felt quite sorry for her, as she was obviously going through a bad time, but there was nothing much I could do for her.

I offered to send through the money due at the end of November, but she declined and said that she and her mum were pulling together just now, so she would be okay. I also told her that if there was anything else I could do, she should just let me know.

I was at least pleased that she had answered and that I

knew in part what would happen on Sunday night if all went according to plan. It had probably been one of our longest chats to date and it was an amicable one, so I was feeling good about it.

A New Life

Saturday came and went pretty quickly, and on the Sunday, full of excitement, I sent Kerry an early morning text to see how she was doing. No response came until just after 7.30 p.m. when she asked if we were all excited, which of course I was. We exchanged a few messages and it was arranged that we would set off to Glasgow at 9.00 p.m. She was due to start the process of being induced at any point up until 10.00 p.m., so I was all packed and ready to go by 8.00 p.m., though we didn't set off until the arranged time. (When I say packed, I just mean I'd packed the things I thought we'd need for the baby!)

Once at the hospital, we parked up and ended up bumping into Christine, Kerry's mum. She had just been in with Kerry, but she had decided to go home until she was needed, so I chatted with her for a while. She was telling me more about the situation with Kerry and her husband, and the situations that had arisen over the past few weeks. She also invited us to go back to her place where we could wait with her until Kerry called to say she was in advanced labour. We declined and ended up going for a drive around Braehead, though nothing was open. Christine called us not long after we had met and asked again if we wanted to go to her place. It was around midnight when Marc and I decided he could maybe go home, see to the dog and bring her back with him, and I could go to Christine's for a while. So, we drove back to the Southern General. Just as we got into the grounds, Kerry called to ask where we were, so I explained what was happening. Marc dropped me off and then I met Kerry; she was looking very different. Apart from the odd dress sense (she was wearing a dressing gown and boots), she had lost a lot of weight and looked quite gaunt. She was also starting to have contractions and told me that she expected the baby to be out way before 6.00 a.m.

Christine then picked me up from the hospital and took me to her place, where Kerry's sister and cousin, plus another friend, were all sat smoking. We all chatted for a couple of hours, until Marc came back and Christine took me back to the hospital to meet him. I also saw Kerry again and she was in some pain by that stage with the contractions.

The next few hours were a bit of a blur; me, Marc and Keira sat in the car, tried to sleep, drove about, went to a 24-hour Asda for some snacks and I had a breakfast burger at McDonalds. We eventually ended up back at the hospital at 6.30 a.m., where we bumped into Christine and Kerry's sister again. They had been told that Kerry was about to go into the delivery suite, so we all walked into the hospital together.

Christine explained to the staff who we all were and the two women were shown to the delivery room. Marc and I were shown to the 'Quiet Room' at the end of the corridor, which felt quite odd. It was obviously a 'bad news' room – dim lighting, a remembrance book and a TV with no available plug socket. So, we sat in there for a few minutes and Christine came down to tell us that Kerry was at 4 cm, so it could be a couple of hours. No sooner had she said that, Kerry's sister burst into the room, telling us that the baby was about to arrive. My heart suddenly started racing, not knowing what to do or say, and Christine ran back out of the room.

Then, just five minutes later, Christine appeared again and said, 'Congratulations, you've just had a daughter!' I was elated! She told me I was to go and cut the cord and I suddenly became a nervous and emotional wreck. We walked up the corridor and into the delivery room, and there she was! Wow! This little thing laid out on the edge of the bed with some blood around her, squealing a little. I was in love – she was beautiful!

This was all a bit of a rushed moment; the nurse put some clamps on the cord and I used some quite blunt scissors to cut between them (I have to admit, it felt like I was trying to cut through a bit of fatty gristle with the bluntest scissors ever!), and my job was done. Kerry was looking quite drawn and asked if she could hold the baby. I told her that she could and then the nurse asked if I wouldn't mind leaving as they had to deliver the placenta, so I went back to the room in tears. Christine followed me halfway and gave me a hug, and then I went in to Marc, told him she was beautiful and we hugged for ages. So, that was that – at 6.56 a.m., my lovely little daughter was born.

After trying to compose myself, I called Mum to tell her the news and couldn't hold back the tears. But, my first words were, 'She's beautiful,' and I told her what I could. I asked her to tell my brother and sister and then tried to compose myself again.

It was only a few minutes later that Christine came down again and said we were to be taken to a different room with the baby; it was the delivery room next to Kerry's, so we were ushered in and waited there. Christine told us that Kerry was having some difficulties and they were struggling to deliver the placenta. Then, this little bundle of joy was brought into the room by Kerry's sister and handed to me. She was just lovely; her faced looked a bit battered because of the quick delivery and she was looking a bit stressed, but she was just lovely and I held on to her for quite some time, walking around the room. Marc also had a good hold and we agreed on the name – Mollie! It seemed to suit her and we were both happy with it. So, Mollie Anna Johnston Rigby she was going to be.

We were in the room for quite a while getting to know Mollie. She was mainly quiet and had a mix of thinly spread blonde and brown hair, longish legs and a very pink face. I couldn't at that stage see any resemblance to me, but everyone else assured me there was. I loved her all the same anyway; she was just a perfect little bundle.

It was quite a while before a nurse came in and she talked us through what was going to happen. I was to feed Mollie and wind her, and then she would get a vitamin K injection to help with blood clotting. Then we might end up in the neonatal ward from where we would be discharged as long as all was okay.

Feeding Mollie felt good; she drank quite a lot of the milk I gave her and winding her seemed easy as well. This also seemed to stop her whingeing, which was a good thing.

After a while, the same nurse brought us some coffee and then took us up to the neonatal unit, where we were given our own room. In there, we met countless people all with different roles to play, and Mollie was given hearing tests, a full check-up, blood was taken and more food was given. Diane Paterson came in to say hello and we thanked her for her input into the process, and also Kathleen, one of the social workers, turned up later in the day to make sure we were okay.

We had been told that we would be allowed to take Mollie home as soon as the nurses were satisfied that all her bodily functions were in good working order. By about 3 p.m., the only one that we were still awaiting evidence for was her ability to poo! Not that it was something I really wanted to witness, but after so long, I was urging her to do one just so we could get out of there, and home to Edinburgh.

Thankfully, one of the nurses came in and said some babies don't manage to poo so quickly, so we should go home, and if nothing happened within the next 24 hours, we should give them a ring.

That was it then – we were free to go, and start life over with my little girl! After managing to get her into a cute furry ski-suit type thing while she was fast asleep, we buckled her into the car seat, and off we went. Marc went to get the car, and I carried Mollie out of the hospital through the rain and to her first car journey. It was such an odd feeling, having 100% responsibility for this little bundle, and really not having much of a clue what I would do with her when we got home! Nonetheless, off we went, and proceeded to spend what seemed like an eternity battling through rush-hour traffic to get home by about 7 p.m. I clearly remember saying 'welcome home' to her as we walked through the door. She didn't respond.

That first night was full of feelings of pride, achievement, love, responsibility and a certain element of fear. But, as the night went on, and I fed her a couple of times, I started to think that being a dad, at least at this stage, wasn't really going to be too difficult.

The past 24 hours had really taken it out of me, though. I had probably managed the best part of an hour's sleep since we left Edinburgh the previous day, and by 11 p.m. we were all in bed. Mollie was asleep in her carrycot in our bedroom, and I drifted off in record time, having checked numerous times that she was still breathing.

I woke up the following morning at about 7 a.m., feeling quite bizarre but well-rested, and I did wonder why Mollie hadn't woken during the night. Surely I can't be so lucky as to have a child who sleeps though the night so soon? Nope, sadly not, It turned out Marc had been up with her in the night, and I hadn't heard a thing!

Living with a Baby!

There were times during the first three months of Mollie's life when I found it hard to believe that she had finally arrived. Being off work for those three months, I spent most of every day with her: feeding, changing nappies, interacting with her more and more when she was awake (which by the end of the three months was most of the day) and generally doing what any other new parent would do. I thoroughly enjoyed myself and I think I did a good job, although nobody told me so.

Every week, I would take Mollie to the clinic run by the health visitors from my GP practice so that she could be weighed and also to ask any questions if there was something I wasn't too sure about. These were always rushed visits; the clinic, held in the Church Hall on Saxe Coburg place, was usually jam-packed full of women, breast-feeding and talking about their experiences with their babies, and I didn't feel a part of that at all. My usual routine was to go in, get Mollie out of her pram or car seat as quickly and quietly as possible, strip her down to her vest, weigh her and then do everything backwards until we got out of there, in the hope that she wouldn't wake up or feel too aggrieved by the fact she was nearly naked in a cold church hall! Not that I minded her being awake, but I just didn't want her to start screaming due to the cold. I sometimes chatted with the staff there, who were always pleasant and supportive, and on the odd occasion I chatted to whoever was using the scales next to me, but it was never a long, drawn-out affair. I was generally only out of the house for about twenty minutes or so.

Christmas was obviously very different that year. We had planned to have Christmas Day at home with Mollie and although we did the usual festive things like the big dinner,

146

some drinks and lots of TV, it was all built around Mollie's routine. She was only six weeks old at this point and really didn't have a clue what was going on. We opened her presents for her, took some pictures and just had a chilled-out day.

The next day, we had to head down to see my family, which wasn't particularly fun, although it was always nice to see the folks. We were staying at my sister's house overnight, in my nephew Callum's room, and obviously everybody just wanted to spend time with Mollie, so we were pretty much redundant for the time we were there. We generally just sat around and chatted, ate loads of food, had a couple of walks, saw some relatives very briefly and that was that! I was glad to get home when we did on 28 December.

Rebecca then came down on 29 December and stayed with us until the New Year. It was a bit cramped in the flat to say the least, but it was good to have her around, and also to have someone to look after Mollie every now and again when Marc and I wanted to nip out. New Year's Eve was again very different; there was no partying or frivolities. The four of us sat in and had some drinks and then, just before midnight, we all headed up to Inverleith Park with a bottle of vodka, diet Irn Bru and a bottle of bubbly stored underneath Mollie's pram. Then we stood there in the park amongst the crowds watching the fireworks going off from the castle whilst Mollie was wrapped up warmly and sleeping soundly through the whole thing. It was nice – different but nice. Back home again, we were all in bed by 1.00 a.m., as I think both Rebecca and Marc were feeling the effects of the alcohol a bit too strongly.

New Year's Day was another lazy day. I made dinner and we all sat about watching TV and playing a few games on the Wii to pass the time. By the time New Year had come and gone, I was starting to realise that I was just about halfway through my time off work and was dreading going back. I felt as if I'd really been wasting my time off with Mollie as we hadn't really done much, but there wasn't much she could do at that age. Plus, we'd had some really bad weather for most of December and going out with the pram was pretty treacherous; it was very, very cold, the pavements weren't cleared and the snow created its own obstacle course with lumps and bumps all over the place. Driving wasn't much better either and Marc ended up taking my car to work for a few days as it was better than his for driving in the snow. So, I was more or less housebound for a while.

The Parental Order

One achievement over the New Year was putting in the application for the parental order with Edinburgh Sheriff Court. We'd had some communication from the lawyers about this and they had suggested they manage it as, in their words, many things can go wrong. They also said they could do it for the cheap figure of £600 (!). I decided I would try to manage it myself, as I really couldn't afford to plough any more money into this whole process. I managed to find the right forms and posted them off at New Year to the court after talking the process through with one of their administrators.

This whole process actually ran pretty smoothly. Maureen McGowan was appointed as court reporter and it was her job to visit us and Kerry to ensure that all was above board and that Mollie was in a safe environment. She came to see us at the start of February and basically just asked us to talk her through the process we had gone through, tell her a bit about ourselves and also our relationship with Kerry. We were positive about the whole thing and it seemed to be a productive meeting. Maureen said she had arranged to see Kerry the following week and may need to come back and see us again. But that wasn't necessary; seemingly, all had gone well in Glasgow, so Maureen could put her report in to the court and that was that.

The court hearing was set for 23 February on Chambers Street, and I really couldn't wait until it was all over. That would be another major milestone in the whole process.

The week of 14 February was my last week off work with Mollie and also the week she was to start her settling-in sessions at the Edinburgh Nursery on East London Street. I wasn't sure how I felt about this, but we finally got to the first session on the Wednesday and she was in there for just an hour. I had the option to stay with her, but after a few minutes I was fairly reassured that she would be looked after, so I went off for a walk. It was odd not having Mollie, even for that hour, and I wasn't quite sure what to do with myself, so I just went into a few shops and was back early to pick her up. She was fine and I think she had just been cuddled by one of the staff for the hour.

The next day, she was in for two hours and on the Friday, she was there for three. It was all okay except that on the Friday she'd been a bit upset, possibly from all the noise going on in there, although she settled again by the time I got her home. That Friday was a very odd one, knowing it was my last day off before going back to work the following Monday. You would think I would have done something to make the most of it, but I couldn't think of what to do! When Mollie was in nursery, I just wandered aimlessly around Princes Street, eating and shopping, but that was it – nothing more exciting than that, apart from a quick haircut, which I admit, isn't exciting at all!

I was due to start back at work on the following Monday and I was dreading it. But, that morning, we managed to get ourselves sorted and Mollie was in nursery by 8.30 a.m. I dropped her off that day and she seemed fine with it, so I felt a little reassured. Work, as it turned out, was pretty mundane; I had a few catch-up chats with colleagues and settled back in to find that really nothing much had changed, apart from some things that had taken a step backwards. To say that progress was limited would be an overstatement: when I left work in November, I had worked furiously to make sure that all of my projects were going according to plan so that in my time away, many would be concluded by colleagues in my absence. Sadly, when I returned, most of them had drawn to a halt, so to say that nothing had changed was pretty much correct.

As that first week went on, I started to have some small doubts about the nursery and the competence of some of the staff in there. On the Tuesday, I had called to see how she was doing and they told me that she had had diarrhoea twice and that if it happened again, she would need to be collected from the nursery. I called the health visitor to chat this through with them, as I knew Mollie always had runny poo, and from what they had said, this didn't seem any different. After a chat with them and Marc, we agreed Marc would explain when he picked Mollie up that she was fine and that she wasn't ill.

The Wednesday of that week was the day of the parental order hearing at court. So, we both had the morning off work and after dropping Mollie off again, made our way to the court. We had no idea what to expect, but there really had been no need to worry. Mary Hughes, the administrator who had been looking after our case, came into court with us and soon enough, we were joined by the sheriff and his clerk. It was literally over in minutes. The Sheriff commented that it was nice to be doing something so positive and that the report he had been sent was all fine, so he granted us the parental order, and that was that – apart from him suggesting we have our photo taken with him! This was quite funny really; he suggested that we stand on the bench (not a bench as we all know it, but the top raised bit of the courtroom) with him so that Mary could take the picture of the three of us, so that is what happened. It was all quite embarrassing, but we were out of there shortly afterwards.

Funny to think that such a long, drawn-out surrogacy process was over within minutes, with what seemed like a brief, informal hearing where nothing happened. Still, it was done and dusted, and we were now solely responsible for Mollie; the positive thing here was that Kerry had no responsibility for Mollie any more and her involvement was over. I just had to arrange for the final chunk of money to be sent to her, which I said I would do the following week.

*   *   *

I realise that throughout my writing, I've been less than positive about Kerry. She has been very difficult to deal with throughout this whole process, and after the Parental Order was granted, my sense of relief at not having to rely on her for anything else, ever again, was immense.

Having said that, I should acknowledge that despite all the problems we have had with her, she has done a fantastic thing for us. Without Kerry, I may not ever have been able to realise my dream of becoming a dad. Having gone through so many women, so to speak, in trying to make this thing work, I really was getting to the end of my tether. Maybe if Kerry hadn't worked out, I would have gone through a whole long line of potentials, and ended up with nothing. So, for that, and for what she did for us, I will be eternally grateful.

I will still never really know the true motivation Kerry had for doing this in the first place. Whether it was financial, or whether she had other reasons is probably irrelevant now, as at the end of the day, all our motivations were realised as far as I am aware.

Contact with Kerry had been limited since Mollie was born. It picked up again when the Parental Order process was under way, at which point she was friendly towards me, via her text messages. She had said in various messages that she was going to move abroad, relocate to the south of England, then buy herself a new house and a new car; her aspirations seemed to be different each time she was in touch. I do understand that she had some struggles in her life, most recently with her husband, and she would now be the single mother of three young children, a situation I wouldn't envy at all. But, it wasn't for me to get involved in any of that. We had agreed at the outset that once any child was born, there wouldn't be any personal contact between her and the child. We could maybe arrange for her to be sent the odd photograph every now and again if she asked, but there was certainly nothing formally agreed about anything, and that was the way I wanted it to stay. We no longer needed to be a part of each other's lives; she would go her way, and we went ours.

A New Home

In the run up to Christmas and New Year, things had started to get more than a little cramped in our Stockbridge flat. Presents for Mollie had just about filled one corner of the lounge, she had been accumulating more and more clothes, toys, teddy bears, and we were starting to feel like we had outgrown the place quicker than expected. But, we knew from the outset that moving into the flat was really just an interim measure.

We had had some discussion about moving house, and the flat had been on the market for quite some time with no success at all. The longer-term plan had been to sell the flat, and use the money from the sale as a deposit for a new, much bigger place, somewhere in Edinburgh. Despite dropping the price a couple of times, we only had a handful of viewers, and only the one offer, which was way below our asking price. So, early in the New Year, we took some trips out to look at new housing developments where we could potentially part-exchange the flat against a bigger property. We knew even then we might struggle to find somewhere affordable, but nonetheless we had to do something to get out of the flat. The only other option would be to rent out the flat, and then rent a bigger place for ourselves, but this wouldn't have been ideal either.

We did find some lovely new houses within the city itself, but sadly the ones we really liked were too far out of our price range. A new development on the site of the old Queen Margaret's University would have been perfect for us, but the £400k asking price for the house we would have wanted was probably about double what we were expecting to have to pay.

In late January, we went to visit a few developments down in East Lothian and Midlothian. Both were a little too far out of the city for our liking, but the houses were affordable, and the figures for part exchange would work. We'd seen some nice places in Dalkeith and Prestonpans, and were heading down the route towards buying one when Marc found an advert for a house in a village called Wallyford, just round the corner from Musselburgh. I had to admit I had never even heard of the place before, but we went along with an open mind to see what the place was like.

The new development we found there was actually quite a nice one, stuck onto the side of the main village, which seemed mainly to be a typical old mining village. The house itself, once we managed to find it, was in a very quiet corner of the development, three stories, back and front gardens, detached garage, nice sized rooms, and altogether lovely! It was also one of the last two houses to be sold on the development, and bearing that in mind, we agreed to buy it there and then, signed the paperwork with the saleswoman, and hoped to God it would all work out.

Buying the place brought about so many hoops to jump through, that at some stages we thought it was all going to go pear shaped. Mortgages were not too easy to come by, both because of the recession, but also because between us we already had twelve other mortgages on investment properties. Our broker finally managed to secure one, and we thought that from that point, it was all systems go.

We were aiming for a completion date of 31 March 2011, the missives were signed and concluded, and then two days before the move, the developers called to say they couldn't accept the Stockbridge flat in part exchange because there was a statutory notice on the building in relation to minor roof repairs! It took about twenty frantic phone calls, a few heated exchanges with the developers and our solicitors, until finally we made them realise they can't back out of the part exchange because contractually they had already signed up to it. So, all systems go again. Phew!

Rebecca came down from Aberdeen and she was such a big help. She agreed to stay in the flat with Mollie while we started the moving process, first getting everything out of storage and taking it to the new house, and then on the next day, moving all our belongings from the flat into the new place, before then having to clean and tidy the flat and handing the keys over to the developers. It was a massive relief to be out of there bearing in mind the troubles we had had getting us to that stage. It was also great to be making a fresh start in our new family-sized home.

Rebecca stayed with us for most of the following three weeks. Marc and I had some time off work to get the new place looking good, putting fixtures and fittings up, etc. and getting to know the local area.

I had managed to find a new nursery for Mollie a few weeks before we moved, and had a place booked in there for her to start full time from 18 April.

On Friday 15 April, a day I was working from home, I took Mollie into her new nursery in Musselburgh for her settling-in session. This place was very different to the last one: much bigger, more open-plan and thankfully it had its own car park, so there would be none of the hassle of trying to park nearby whilst dodging the traffic wardens. She was due in there at 10.00 a.m. and as usual, I arrived early and met with a number of the staff, all of whom seemed nice and pleasant.

They immediately took to Mollie and one of the staff started giving her a bottle of milk while I filled out some more paperwork and found out some more about the routine there. After half an hour, I left Mollie with them and headed home for the plumber to arrive. By 12.00 p.m. I was back there again; they said she had been absolutely fine, had taken all of her milk and they had kept her occupied for most of the time, although she had fallen asleep just before I arrived to collect her, so she was in a cot having a snooze. As usual, I felt bad for waking her up and we went home for the afternoon, with me trying to get some work done and keep Mollie entertained.

The following Monday, she started there full-time. I'd been panicking about the commute to work, as we could only drop her off at 8.00 a.m., though for the past two weeks we had been leaving the house a lot earlier to miss the traffic. It was fine, though; we arrived at the nursery at about 7.50 a.m. and left there at about 8.10 a.m., as they were late in opening the doors. She seemed quite content when we left her there. Both Marc and I went in with her and left her in the arms of one of the staff, who told us to call during the day, which I did late morning to be told that she was just fine.

This was the first day that we had left Keira in the house all day by herself, so the guilt for Mollie was doubled with the guilt we felt for Keira. I expected that she would be fine, although we wouldn't know until we made it home that night.

All was okay; Keira had been fine and Mollie had had a good day at the nursery, and all of the staff were singing her praises. Seemingly, she had been full of fun all day long, so my mind was put at rest.

After two weeks of the new nursery, everything settled down. Mollie was doing really well and the staff there just loved her. But it was a bit of a pain in the mornings, waiting for the nursery doors to open, as sometimes they were a bit late, and that made for a frustrating rush to work.

Marc and I were travelling together in my car at this time; he was dropping me off first and getting to work just about on time every day, and then leaving early to pick me up and then get to nursery. I could sense he was becoming frustrated with it sometimes, but there wasn't much we could do about that, unless we both started taking our cars to work, which would then double the fuel costs.

We did shorter working weeks for those first two weeks, as it was Easter, and we also had my family up to the new house for the first time, which was lovely. It was the first time I'd seen my dad walk since his operation the year before, so I was doubly pleased to see him.

Solids

We started to give Mollie something other than baby milk just after the four-month stage. This had initially been baby rice and we then progressed to rusks, mashed-up with water, and then mashed-up with some banana, which she seemed to like. It was fun trying to feed her, sitting in her bouncy chair; at the start, most of the food tended to end up either all over her face, on her hands or on her bib, but after a while she seemed to enjoy it. This was only an evening thing for us at the start, so once we got in from work, we were giving her some food, having ours and then giving her some milk.

We'd been given a few jars of proper baby food, so we also started giving her these, which were more savoury than her first meals – cheesy parsnip with apple or cauliflower cheese – and again she seemed to take to these.

Once she had been at the new nursery for a couple of weeks, the staff told us that she was starting to get upset at mealtimes, as she was just getting her bottle but the other children were being fed proper (pureed) food. So, we agreed that from the following week (starting on 2 May), they could give her meals along with everyone else, as long as they were pureed.

We decided that we would get her used to more food that weekend, so started her on three meals a day from the Friday morning; it was the day of William and Kate's Royal Wedding (a day off work for both of us) so we had plenty of time to feed her. By the end of the weekend, she had sampled the delights of baby porridge with raspberry, sweet potato, more cauliflower cheese, more cheesy parsnip and breakfast rice, and she seemed to take to it all okay, though it did seem to play havoc with her bowels on the Friday night, when she was obviously out of sorts and just wouldn't settle at all. The rest of the weekend she was fine, though, and was quite happily eating everything in sight, as well as her milk, although she wasn't taking all of that as the solid stuff must have been filling her up.

On the Monday morning, we confirmed to the nursery that they could give her meals and snacks along with everyone else, as long as we could monitor it as we went along.

Teeth and Other Developments

Mollie was teething on and off for the spring months and by mid-May, she had a tiny bit of tooth showing through her bottom gum. She seemed to be coping with it okay and it was weird to feel it scrape against the spoon as I was feeding her.

The last weekend of May, we had decided to take Mollie down to my parents for the weekend. Mum had been keen to have her at the house, although we didn't really want to have to stay there. It would be a case of 'pass the Mollie' all weekend, but it gave us an opportunity to get away and have some fun by ourselves. So, on the Friday we headed down to Freckleton, said hi to the family, got Mollie settled and when she was having her bath, we left and headed over to Manchester for the weekend.

I was almost tearful when we left her; this was the first time I had spent a night without her since she was born and although I knew she would be well looked after, it was still a bit of a wrench walking out of the door. Needless to say, once we got to Manchester, I was fine with it. I did call Mum later on to check she was okay and she was, of course.

The weekend was a bit of a drunken one. We were out late on the Friday night and didn't get to sleep until about 6.30 a.m., and the Saturday was almost as bad, except that I seemed to be quite drunk and was actually sick at the end of the night; something that hadn't happened in quite a long time. But, it was good to get away and I was glad not to have to change nappies at 7.30 a.m. with such a bad hangover.

On the Sunday morning, before heading back to see my folks, I called Mum who told me that Mollie had actually cut a tooth. I had expected something to happen that weekend. When we eventually got back, we found that the tooth hadn't really grown much at all over the weekend. I was quite chuffed that it still didn't look much like a tooth – still just little white bits poking through her gum – and I hadn't missed anything.

Her two bottom teeth eventually came through properly and by mid-June, they were well and truly out. They were also very painful, especially when I had to put teething gel in her mouth and she bit hard on my fingers!

June was a positive month for Mollie in terms of her development. As well as her two bottom teeth coming through, another one at the side of them started to appear as well. Oddly, none of the top ones were through by the end of the month; we had expected these to follow the bottom ones quite quickly.

Mollie, by this stage, was able to sit up pretty much on her own. We could put her on her play mat on the floor with her toys and she would happily sit there and play. Her general approach was to put everything in her mouth; obviously she was still teething, but it was good to be able to watch her sit up at least. She was also becoming very vocal; she would babble away about nothing and every now and again we would hear the word 'Dada' in the middle of a rant. I was convinced that she was using our name, but Marc was having none of it. It used to make me laugh, though.

June was also the month in which Mollie had her first real tummy bug. She had been a bit off colour one day and then at the weekend, all hell broke loose – well, hell in terms of nappy hell. We realised there was a problem when out in the car one day, she had filled her nappy and it had leaked out all over her clothes and the car seat. This then continued for the best part of five days. Marc caught the bug as well, so there was one day when they were both having projectile emissions from behind. For the most part, Mollie was fine in herself, apart from vomiting a couple of times. She was quite happy, though, and still slept well, although she must have been slightly awake some nights to have been able to fill her nappies so well before I went in to get her in the mornings.

That reminds me – the other great thing about June was how much I really looked forward to getting Mollie up in the morning. Although it was all still a bit of a rush in the mornings, I loved going into her room and seeing the big smile on her face and her legs kicking about excitedly when she saw me, and also how when I picked her up, she held onto me quite closely until we were downstairs. It was such a fantastic start to the day.

Oh, and one final further development was food. Yep, June was the month when Mollie started to eat some good old home cooking. By the end of the month she had had bangers and mash, Lasagne, steak pie and mash, haggis and steak pie and mash, cheese butties and the list goes on. But, it was all going really well. We also saved a fortune on those little jars of baby food. There were a couple of occasions that some of it was a bit too lumpy for her, but she was doing so well. She even managed to feed herself some banana, melon and strawberry. I was such a proud dad!

Forty and Beyond

My fortieth birthday quickly came around, and on 9 August 2011 there it was. I was forty years old. Marc turned forty-three on the same day and Mollie was there to celebrate it with us.

The day itself was a fairly quiet one, with Rebecca down staying with us. I woke up after a long lie-in bed at 11.00 a.m. and found that all sorts of banners and balloons had been plastered to the walls, and there was one big banner on the front fence loudly announcing my new age. It brought a smile to my face at least.

I did think a few times that day that I should be feeling quite old. I remember when I was young, thinking that forty was ancient, but I still felt nineteen years old in my head. My birthday came and went without a bang and all was back to normality by the end of the week.

It was the following week that our routine changed; Rebecca was now staying with us for three days a week and looking after Mollie for those three days. This was all intended to save us a fortune in nursery fees, but it didn't really work out that way. Marc wanted Rebecca to be paid something for looking after Mollie and also reimbursed for any travel costs back and forth to Aberdeen. This effectively wiped out any savings I was going to make. I say 'I' as Marc didn't pay anything towards Mollie's fees, and even though he was saving money by not having to travel to Aberdeen every fortnight, he didn't feel he should be paying anything towards what Rebecca was getting.

Anyhow, this whole new arrangement started with Rebecca arriving on Sunday 14 August and staying with us until the Wednesday.

By this time, we had also booked our time away. We now

had a long weekend planned for the end of August, when we would leave Mollie with Mum and Dad for the weekend. We were due to go to Manchester. Unbeknown to us when we booked, it was Gay Pride in Manchester that weekend, so I was a bit anxious about it, but thought it would be fun. We had also managed to get a week in Mykonos at the end of September, again with Mum having Mollie for the week and us flying out from Manchester. I did sometimes have some pangs of guilt about leaving Mollie, but these soon disappeared once I remembered that half the reason for doing this was so that Mollie and my family could spend time together and get to know each other a lot better. I was still concerned that she would grow up quite distant from her relatives, so this was one way of bridging that gap, albeit quite irregularly.

The long weekend in Manchester was a good one; we had a ball and Mollie and the family all seemed to have a good time together. In fact, when we got back to my parents' house, she didn't even seem overly pleased to see us. Nevertheless, she was happy and jolly as usual and hadn't grown any more teeth this time.

Over the weekend at Pride, we visited a stall manned by people promoting gay surrogacy. The couple sponsoring it were the ones who had been on TV the previous year in a programme about how they had five children through surrogacy, all done in the States. We made an effort to speak to them, but they really didn't seem overly interested in what we had to say. We did take a few leaflets, but most of it didn't tell us anything we didn't already know. Well, at least it passed some time away while it was raining.

Nearly Walking

Back home after our frivolities in Manchester, we both had a short week at work. Marc took ill with a cold and I was only in on the Wednesday and Friday as I worked at home on the Thursday. So, we had lots of time with Mollie and I started to notice a real difference in her, especially in her mobility. By the end of that weekend, she was moving about on the floor (though not quite crawling) and was able to stand up holding herself up, of course with one of us keeping our hands next to her to catch her when she fell. She really was finding her feet, though, and on Sunday 4 September, she finally took a step by herself to get from me to Marc. It was just the one step, but nevertheless it was a start. That day, she also spent a lot of time in the baby walker, which we took out to the driveway, and there she was zooming around in it. Sadly, she kept leaning to one side, which made her go round in circles, bumping into the back of Marc's car as she went, but she really was moving and by the look on her face, she was enjoying every minute of it. It was a real pleasure to watch and I really couldn't wait to see her on her feet properly. Knowing my luck, that would probably happen while we were away on holiday. I promised myself at that point that I would do all I could to get her walking before then.

At ten months she still wasn't talking (I know – I expect too much!) although she was regularly saying 'Dadadadadadada', which I obviously interpreted as 'Daddy' and she did mutter away using other more incomprehensible noises. She was coming on, though, and I was as pleased as Punch.

Soon enough, it was time for us to go on holiday. We headed down south to Freckleton and then flew out to Mykonos, leaving Mollie with the family for the week. I'd been a bit worried about all this, not least because that week

Mollie had had an ear infection, and it had only just cleared up by the time we were ready to get away. I'd gone back to the doctor with her to double check that it was all better, as I didn't want Mum panicking about having to deal with a grumpy child all week.

Well, once away, we had a ball and thoroughly enjoyed ourselves. The weather was great, we met some really nice people and generally made the best of it. In fact, I needed another holiday by the time we got home. When we were away, I had missed Mollie a lot and I'd phoned every day to see how she was doing. I also made sure that my sister sent some pictures through so that we could see how she was getting on.

It was lovely getting back to Freckleton and seeing Mollie, and I was amazed to see how much she seemed to have changed in such a short space of time. She didn't seem over-excited to see us, but I think that was because she had been having such a good time with the family. Mum and Dad had really enjoyed having her and although Mum was shattered, I think she loved it.

We were back home to Wallyford on the Saturday and in no time at all, it felt as if we had never been away. The usual routine started: back to work (which I just didn't enjoy at all) and Mollie was back to nursery by the Thursday. Unfortunately, she picked up a bug at nursery that week and on the Sunday, she started with a bad dose of the runs, to the point that it was coming out of her nappy and all over everywhere. Rebecca arrived to look after her on the Sunday and it didn't improve. I caught the bug, as did Rebecca and on the Tuesday, Mollie took a turn for the worse, as she was very dehydrated. I had to dash home as Rebecca was worried about how Mollie was doing. Yet another trip to the doctor's told us that we had to get her to drink a lot of liquid, otherwise we would have to take her to hospital. So, we did all we could and ended up using an oral syringe to keep her drinking, which did the trick.

It wasn't until Saturday that the runs finally cleared up. Rebecca had ended up staying the whole week as she didn't fancy going home on the train with a dose of the runs, so we managed a night out on the Saturday night and after that, the usual routine fell back into place.

On Monday 17 October, Mollie decided to walk yet again! This time, it was a real independent walk; Rebecca was holding Mollie up on her feet, but she was trying to get to me while I was kneeling on the floor. So, Rebecca let go and Mollie just walked right over to me, taking about four steps on the way. We all cheered loudly and were over the moon, although I don't think Mollie really knew what had happened, and we couldn't get her to do it again.

The following Saturday, Mollie had her first haircut – nothing overly exciting; we just took her to the place next to the nursery where they trimmed her fringe and it was over in two minutes. We kept some of the hair, though, although I'd no idea what I was going to do with it.

One Year On

On 15 November 2011, my beautiful daughter reached the grand old age of one. It was something I had really been looking forward to and just seemed like a major milestone for me; not only had I become a dad, but I'd also proved to be a capable one as well, having made sure she made it safely through her first year.

My parents and brother, as well as Rebecca, came to visit for the weekend before Mollie's birthday and we had a little informal gathering. It wasn't a major event, but it was good; I made some chilli and some stovies, and we all sat and ate and drank and chatted. As expected, Mollie got a load of presents from all and sundry, but we were already running out of space in our house to put anything at all. Still, she seemed to enjoy herself and although she probably didn't have a clue what was going on, she was happy enough.

It was now when my reflections over the whole process really started to happen. I had been through probably the most challenging, emotional, worrying, unsettling and exciting period of my life, but I started to look back and analyse what had happened, the events that had taken place since I first discussed the possibility of becoming a dad with Marc, and the hurdles we had overcome along the way.

I had learned a lot about myself in the previous few years. Some good things, some not so good, but it was such a big process to go through that my overriding thought was that, if I hadn't been me and remained true to myself (for all my faults), then things would probably have worked out very differently in the end.

I have known for a long time that I always look for the good in people. If someone tells me something, I am generally always inclined to believe them, unless I have some objective evidence which tells me I shouldn't. It's this area where I seem to differ most between my professional and personal life. At work now, and in my career in Human Resources for the past fifteen years or so, I've had responsibility for large teams, dealt with some very difficult casework, and interviewed hundreds of job applicants. At work, it's easy – I have no problem in assessing someone's suitability for a role, in working out whether someone really has the skills, experience or personality traits I'm looking for. It's very rare that I've been wrong in all these types of decisions, and in fact I can only pinpoint one bad recruitment decision in all of my career. But, in my personal life, and specifically in trying to have a child, the emotional issues surrounding the decisions I have been faced with making have severely clouded my judgement.

Looking back through the whole process, I have in the past made excuses for the decisions I've made. For example Katie – she was, on the face of it at least, friendly, sincere and fun. She was also down to earth, a quality I really appreciate in people, whatever aspect of my life they come into. But, when it really came down to it, how was I to know that she was purely financially motivated when she initially agreed to move forward through a surrogacy process? Meeting and talking to potential surrogates isn't quite as straightforward as interviewing someone for a job. You can't be formal, you can't really read from a list of questions, you can't ask them to fill out a personality questionnaire, and worst of all, you can't even ask them to take a lie-detector test. When I think personally about Katie, the first of a long line of women who potentially could have had a child for me (I discounted Karen as she was a no-hoper), there was so much I should have done to help me work out just what I needed to know before I ever agreed to make a start with her.

She had initially said she had volunteered to be an egg donor, but was subsequently asked if she would be a

170

surrogate. It's a bit of a major step from one to the other, and I never asked her if surrogacy was something she really wanted to be involved in. I never asked if, actually, she was happy to carry someone else's child and give it away when it was born. She seemed to be going along with it, but there was never any 'I really want to do this because ...' type of conversation. On my part, I just accepted that, because she was there entertaining the whole idea, she was up for it. Big mistake.

With Denise, I suppose it wasn't quite so clear cut. She had (apparently) been through part of the process before, and it hadn't worked. However, as events turned out, she didn't have that supportive partner that she initially convinced us she had. It became obvious towards the end of our 'relationship' with her that she and her partner weren't as committed to the process as they needed to be. Despite the constant reassurances I had from Emma that all was going to be okay with Denise, I don't suppose I ever had 100% confidence that it would be, and my gut instinct was right. Nonetheless, I carried on hoping all would be fine, up to the point where that final call came to say she would no longer do it.

I expect even by this stage, most people would be thinking, 'I need to take a different approach here.' But no, not me, I just carried on regardless. Along came Jemma, and again I just jumped headlong into the 'getting to know you' process, and took her at face value. Granted, she wasn't my cup of tea in many ways, but when someone says to you, 'I'd love to have a child for you,' you think to yourself that surely nobody could lie about such an important, life-changing agreement. My feelings of doubt about the whole plan were so strong at the stage where Jemma's true levels of commitment were starting to show: doubts about ever finding anyone to do this; serious doubts about my own judgement, and an overwhelming sense that this really was just a pipe dream which would never be realised.

Not sure whether I was a glutton for punishment or not, I just carried on. Yes, I was disheartened, but yet again, when Ana came on the scene and actually went for two lots of IVF treatment, my faith in humanity was restored, and I started to feel certain yet again that one day, I would be the dad I always wanted to be.

I can readily admit that my sense of judgement throughout this whole process was just downright poor. My heart was set on having a child, and that clouded any real ability to objectively judge whether those people who had offered to carry a child were actually the right people. As soon as anyone said yes, I just went with the flow, and had to live with the consequences.

I think that general theme started, unfortunately, when I first went to meet John Gonzalez. Having had knockbacks from all the legitimate surrogacy organisations in the UK, to find someone who would actually help me was, at the time, a massive relief. Faced with no other available options apart from going to the States, it was John, or nothing. Of course, had I waited a few years, I would have seen changes in the legal provisions for discrimination, and would have been able to make use of the real surrogacy organisations that straight couples had been able to use. But, at the outset, I believed John when he said he had managed surrogacy processes for same sex couples in the past, and I trusted him to manage the process for us, in a professional, supportive, understanding way. Sadly, I got it wrong, on all counts, and looking back I find it hard to believe that he had ever managed the process for any couple, never mind a gay couple. Still, who knows what would have happened if I hadn't found him in the first place? The dealings we had with Emma after John was jailed were pretty frustrating to say the least. She was inconsistent, annoyingly happy (all the time, even when delivering bad news), and failed on a number of occasions to do what she promised. I never actually made a

172

decision to involve Emma in all this, but it was just a given that she took over from John when he was put away. Having said that, it was she who orchestrated the whole thing with Kerry, arranged the IVF and medication so I should really pass on my thanks to her, albeit reluctantly. I often wonder what she is doing now; whether she has managed to find a place in the surrogacy business to keep her occupied, or whether she has decided she's really not suited to any of that, and has taken a normal job instead. I'm hoping it's the latter, for everyone's sake.

On the positive side, I have come to realise that I am at least determined. It was a difficult enough decision to make in embarking on this whole process. It's easy enough to decide you want a child, but not so easy when you agree to start down that path as a same sex couple. Sometimes I astounded even myself when, after each failure, I picked myself up, dusted myself off, and carried on regardless. In some respects, it was a lonely experience a lot of the time. I hadn't really mentioned much about it to anyone as I had decided that I wouldn't get anyone's hopes up until I knew there was a reason to, i.e., that a baby was on its way. My support network in Edinburgh was very limited, and discussions about it at home for the most part had been brief. So, to carry on, even when I was expecting yet more disappointment, heartache, failure and lies, and to have to deal with much of it on my own, was something for which I thank my own determination.

Had I waited a few years to start down this path, things may have worked out very differently, or not at all. Had I decided to go to the States to do this, I may have had a child earlier than I did. If I had doubted John's ability to support me through this in the first place, where would I be now? All of these questions I really can't answer.

The one question I can answer is 'Have I any regrets?' and my answer is 'No.' For all the issues I faced, the challenges, the turmoil, now that I have this beautiful little girl in my life, the history pales into insignificance. Every day when I see her face, I simply see my little girl. Every day when we play, sing, eat our meals, I see what I have always wanted right in front of me, and really don't pay much regard to how she got here. She's here, and that's all that matters.

And Life Goes on

I could write for days and days about my experiences with Mollie. Life since her first birthday has been full of fun. I expect that most people experience the same things, so there's nothing new in much of it. New to me, yes, but probably pretty run of the mill as parenting goes.

We reached a number of milestones in the second year of her life: she started to walk properly on 18 December 2011, her communication skills came on quite rapidly (her first word was o-oh), she was potty trained, knew most people's names, and began to watch telly, for only some brief spells, but it meant at least she had some quiet moments. We also took her along to her first Gay Pride in Edinburgh in June 2012, which I think she thoroughly enjoyed.

I had started to feel like I had my own little family, and that really was lovely. I had previously constantly worried about what Marc's involvement with Mollie was going to be as she grew and needed more attention. In the early months, once I was back at work, we had had some disagreements about who should be getting up with her in the morning and get her ready for nursery. It ended up being me for the most part, but after a while Marc agreed to alternate with me, which meant I was able to get a little more sleep than I had been.

For the most part, everything works out well for us now. We are both 'Daddy' to her (although we really need to sort that out at some point), she pays me as much attention as Marc, and we enjoy all spending time together. Marc and I have different ideas about the way things should be done, and sometimes we compromise, sometimes we don't. But, it works, and I expect that is the way it will continue.

And one of my initial concerns has disappeared altogether: I had – a long, long time ago – worried about how we would be treated, a family consisting of two dads and one daughter. I am so relieved to say, we have encountered nothing but positivity from everyone we've met. Nursery staff, staff at the doctor's, family, friends, strangers have all been great. Marc's concern about 'the gayness of it all' seems to have disappeared, and life goes on.

Would I do it again? Well, it's a question I've been asked a number of times. Now, despite how much I love my daughter, and have loved every minute she has been here with me, I have to say that the answer is a resounding 'NO'. I know, the results of going through a successful surrogacy process bring the most fantastic gift, but there's no way I'm going through that again. Yes, there are agencies to help, legislation to clear the path of any discrimination, and people like John Gonzalez have no further place in the surrogacy world, but I don't think my heart could take it. For that matter, neither could my bank balance.

Now, I am a dad, and a good one if I say so myself. The rewards Mollie brings to my life have far exceeded my expectations about parenthood. The love she shows me, the cuddles, and laughs. I never knew it would be this good.

1	2	3	4	5	6	7	8	9	10
11	12	13	14	15	16	17	18	19	20
21	22	23	24	25	26	27	28	29	30
31	32	33	34	35	36	37	38	39	40
41	42	43	44	45	46	47	48	49	50
51	52	53	54	55	56	57	58	59	60
61	62	63	64	65	66	67	68	69	70
71	72	73	74	75	76	77	78	79	80
81	82	83	84	85	86	87	88	89	90
91	92	93	94	95	96	97	98	99	100
101	102	103	104	105	106	107	108	109	110
111	112	113	114	115	116	117	118	119	120
121	122	123	124	125	126	127	128	129	130
131	132	133	134	135	136	137	138	139	140
141	142	143	144	145	146	147	148	149	150
151	152	153	154	155	156	157	158	159	160
161	162	163	164	165	166	167	168	169	170
171	172	173	174	175	176	177	178	179	180
181	182	183	184	185	186	187	188	189	190
191	192	193	194	195	196	197	198	199	200
201	202	203	204	205	206	207	208	209	210
211	212	213	214	215	216	217	218	219	220
221	222	223	224	225	226	227	228	229	230
231	232	233	234	235	236	237	238	239	240
241	242	243	244	245	246	247	248	249	250
251	252	253	254	255	256	257	258	259	260
261	262	263	264	265	266	267	268	269	270
271	272	273	274	275	276	277	278	279	280
281	282	283	284	285	286	287	288	289	290
291	292	293	294	295	296	297	298	299	300
301	302	303	304	305	306	307	308	309	310
311	312	313	314	315	316	317	318	319	320
321	322	323	324	325	326	327	328	329	330
331	332	333	334	335	336	337	338	339	340
341	342	343	344	345	346	347	348	349	350
351	352	353	354	355	356	357	358	359	360
361	362	363	364	365	366	367	368	369	370
371	372	373	374	375	376	377	378	379	380
381	382	383	384	385	386	387	388	389	390
391	392	393	394	395	396	397	398	399	400